D0510603

Madeira
& Porto Santo

DIRECTIONS

WRITTEN AND RESEARCHED BY

Matthew Hancock

with additional accounts by

Amanda Tomlin and Jane Gordon

ROUGH
GUIDES

NEW YORK • LONDON • DELHI
www.roughguides.com

Contents

Introduction to

Madeira
& Porto Santo

Ajuzelos, Chamber of Commerce

Surrounded by the warm seas of the Atlantic some 600km off the west coast of Morocco, Madeira is an island of wild mountains, precipitous valleys and sheer cliffs – including some of the highest sea cliffs in the world at Cabo Girão. The island's dramatic scenery makes for some fantastic walking, and it also boasts a diverse array of colourful sub-tropical vegetation, gently cultivated terraces and rocky beaches. Its lesser-known sister island, Porto Santo, has a less dramatic landscape, but compensates with a superb nine-kilometre-long beach.

The island's year-round mild climate, excellent hotel facilities and extremely low levels of crime have long attracted older visitors, though these days a much younger crowd is being lured by the

▲ Fortaleza do Pico, Funchal

When to go

Near-permanent sunshine makes Madeira an all-year destination. Northern Europeans visit mostly in winter, when average maximum daily temperatures are around 20°C. Portuguese visitors predominate in summer (around 24°C), when – despite the modest increase in temperature – the whole island has a more outdoor feel, with cafés moving their tables out onto the streets and every accessible part of coast thronging with bathers. Peak time, however, is over New Year, when hotels hike up their prices by some thirty percent. Other busy times coincide with school holidays, especially Easter and August. Low season is roughly late October to early December and late January to pre-Easter, which also coincides with the wettest months. Outside high summer, rain is possible at any time, though it rarely sets in for long.

Porto Santo has its own climate. Rainfall is very low and most days are dry and sunny, though it can be breezy. On both Madeira and Porto Santo, low cloud, known as *capacete*, sometimes descends from the mountains at around lunchtime, though this usually clears by mid-afternoon and acts as a handy shield against the strongest sun of the day.

island's "green" and healthy credentials. These include excellent *levada* walks along the island's network of irrigation canals, various spa facilities and a growing number of sports, such as golf, deep-sea fishing, diving and surfing.

Madeira and Porto Santo were uninhabited until they were discovered and colonized by Portuguese explorers in the fifteenth century. Thanks to its strategic position on a major shipping route, Madeira soon established itself as an important trading post, linking Portugal with its colonies in Africa and America. In the seventeenth century, the British – Portugal's traditional commercial ally – largely took control of a burgeoning wine trade, leading to a strong British influence on the island's elite. Influential Anglo–Madeiran families

▲ The Lido, Funchal

◀ The mountainous interior, Rabaçal

can be found to this day, but, although English is widely spoken, the population is nearly all of mainland Portuguese descent – the signs, culture and architecture are Portuguese, and so are the superb pastries, powerful coffees and top table wines.

Once one of the poorest parts of Portugal and consequently of Europe, Madeira gained semi-autonomous status within the Portuguese Republic in 1976 and the island has since flourished. Its president has successfully lobbied for EU funds to subsidize new roads, tunnels and building projects that have propelled most of the island firmly into the twenty-first century. These days Madeirans are not only proudly Portuguese, but proudly Madeiran too.

◀ Nossa Senhora de Monte

Madeira's building boom continues, but equal efforts have been made to preserve its natural heritage: the island boasts the greatest concentration of virgin lauraceous forests in the world, and an astonishing 66 percent of the island enjoys protected national-park status. Despite its compact size, there are parts of the island where you feel as though you're in the middle of a magical wilderness.

Madeira & Porto Santo
AT A GLANCE

FUNCHAL

Funchal is the island's historic capital. Very Portuguese in character and architecture, the town has enough museums, sights, restaurants, bars and shops to keep you occupied for at least a week. It's also close to many of the island's top tourist attractions, including Monte, a pretty hilltop town famed for its gardens and dry toboggan run, and Câmara de Lobos, an atmospheric fishing village that Winston Churchill took to his heart.

▼ Jardim Botânico, Funchal

▲ Cable car to Monte

EASTERN MADEIRA

Relatively built up, eastern Madeira's highlights include Machico, the island's first capital; the rocky peninsula of Ponta de São Lourenço, with Madeira's only natural sand beach; and Santo da Serra, home to the island's top golf course. The main resort is Caniço de Baixo, with superb swimming and diving possibilities.

WESTERN MADEIRA

Set among verdant banana plantations, Ribeira Brava and Calheta are the main resorts on the unspoilt western coastline. Calheta boasts an artificial sandy beach and the island's top art centre. The smaller Jardim do Mar and Paúl do Mar have a growing surfing scene, while inland there are superb walks around the wooded valleys of Rabaçal.

◀ Summit, Pico Ruivo

NORTHEASTERN MADEIRA

Highlights in the northeast include Santana, famed for its triangular houses, and the picturesque village of Porto da Cruz. Also in this area, the dramatic peaks of Pico Arieiro and Pico Ruivo, more than 1800m high, offer great walks and fantastic alpine views over the island's coasts.

NORTHWESTERN MADEIRA

The northwest of the island is wild and dramatic, with precipitous hillsides gouged by waterfalls. The main centres here are Porto Moniz, which has invigorating natural sea pools, and São Vicente, one of the island's prettiest villages, close to some weird volcanic grottoes.

PORTO SANTO

Easily accessible by ferry or plane, Porto Santo, Madeira's neighbouring island, is fringed by a sumptuous sandy beach accessible from the pretty town of Vila Baleira.

◀ Porto Santo

Ideas

The big six

Madeira's main sights are readily accessible from any point of the island and can easily be visited during a week's stay. The following give an idea of the diverse attractions available, from historic towns and churches to natural wonders such as towering mountains and sheer cliff faces, not to mention the superb sandy beach on Porto Santo.

▲ Funchal

The only town of any size on Madeira, the attractive capital makes the perfect base for exploring the island.

P.51 ▸ CENTRAL FUNCHAL

▼ Cabo Girão

Whether viewed from the sea or from the top, these vertiginous sea cliffs are a spectacular sight.

P.108 ▸ NORTHWEST OF FUNCHAL

▼ Monte

A hilltop town boasting great views, lush gardens and the island's most sacred church, guarding a venerated statue of the Virgin.

P.93 ▶ MONTE AND NORTHEAST OF FUNCHAL

▲ Machico

With its own little beach and surrounded by banana plantations, historic Machico makes a great alternative base to Funchal.

P.118 ▶ THE SOUTHEAST AND MACHICO

▶ Pico Ruivo

At 1862m high, this mountain peak offers stupendous views across the whole island, often from high above the cloudline.

P.168 ▶ NORTHERN MADEIRA

◀ Porto Santo

Perhaps Europe's best-kept secret, Madeira's sister island has 9km of pristine sands and a famous golf course.

P.176 ▶ PORTO SANTO

Walks

Madeira is rightly famous for its walks. Many of these are along the well-marked *veredas* (paths) which were used by locals to travel from village to village before the road network was constructed. Even more popular are the island's *levada* walks, along the sides of irrigation canals that wend through some of the island's wildest scenery.

▲ Prazeres to Paúl do Mar

Zigzag down one of the west coast's steepest cliffs, with great views en route.

P.142 ▸ THE WEST

▲ Levada do Caldeirão Verde

One of the island's most spectacular *levada* walks, winding through ancient lauraceous forests.

P.167 ▸ NORTHERN MADEIRA

▲ Levada da Central da Ribeira da Janela, Porto Moniz

An attractive, gentle *levada* hike that takes you deep into the rural north.

P.154 ▶ PORTO MONIZ AND THE NORTHWEST

▲ Pico do Arieiro to Pico Ruivo

Madeira's most famous and memorable walk, between two of its highest peaks.

P.170 ▶ NORTHERN MADEIRA

▲ Lorano to Machico

An exhilarating clifftop path high above the north coast.

P.132 ▶ THE EAST AND PORTO DA CRUZ

▶ Rabaçal to 25 Fontes

A beautiful *levada* walk into Madeira's lush woodland heart.

P.143 ▶ THE WEST

Transport

Getting around Madeira – surrounded by the Atlantic, fringed by cliffs and rising inland to 1862m above sea level – has long posed problems to travellers and engineers alike. Over time, many of the island's most challenging features have been ingeniously exploited to provide easy access and highly enjoyable ways of getting from A to B. From dry toboggans to high-tech lifts and cable cars, many of the rides are worth going on for the thrill alone.

▲ Lift to Fajã das Padres

The beachside settlement of Fajã das Padres is reached by a thrilling descent down the cliff face in a glass-fronted lift.

P.108 ▶ NORTHWEST OF FUNCHAL

▲ Santa Maria de Columbo

Get a different perspective on the island on a boat trip from Funchal harbour.

P.198 ▸ ESSENTIALS

▼ Cable car at Achada da Cruz

Not for the faint-hearted, this dizzy descent is an adrenalin-pumping way to see the wild northwest coast.

P.151 ▸ PORTO MONIZ AND
NORTHWESTERN
MADEIRA

▼ Monte toboggan

Traditional basket toboggans are a bizarre, novel and exhilarating way to get down a mountain.

P.97 ▸ MONTE AND NORTHEAST
OF FUNCHAL

▼ Cable car to Monte

The best views over Funchal are from the slowly ascending cable car from the Zona Velha.

P.85 ▸ EASTERN FUNCHAL AND
THE OLD TOWN

Sports and activities

Madeira and Porto Santo boast three top golf courses between them, while Madeira's climate and terrain are also ideal for several other sports. Game fishing is big business, surfing has a dedicated following and an increasing number of companies offer adventure sports, from canyoning to diving. Madeira's pre-eminent sport, however, is football, and the island that produced the silky skills of Cristiano Ronaldo also has teams in Portugal's top division.

▲ **Mountain bikes**

Get off the beaten track on a mountain-bike trip along the spectacular *levada* paths.

P.197 ▶ ESSENTIALS

▲ Diving

Explore sea caverns, wrecks and the clear, deep water, swimming with moray eels, Atlantic rays and mantas.

P.197 ▸ ESSENTIALS

▼ Football

Catch one of Portugal's top teams, Marítimo or Nacional, who entertain the likes of Porto and Benfica.

P.198 ▸ ESSENTIALS

▲ Porto Santo Golf

Porto Santo Golf, on Porto Santo, is rated the best course in this corner of the Atlantic.

P.181 ▸ PORTO SANTO

▶ Surfing

Madeira has a burgeoning reputation as a surfing centre. Jardim do Mar is one of the top places to take to the waves.

P.197 ▸ ESSENTIALS

Viewpoints

The legacy of Madeira's volcanic past is a landscape of peaks and cliffs rising sheer from the ocean floor. Wherever you go you'll find dazzling vistas and dramatic *miradouro* viewpoints. Madeirans love nothing better than taking off for a summer picnic, and there are little wooden benches dotted round some of the island's most scenic spots. At others, you'll be alone to enjoy the view in spectacular solitude.

▲ **Pico do Arieiro**

One of the highest points on the island – conveniently accessible by road for jaw-dropping views.

P.170 ▶ NORTHERN MADEIRA

▲ Boca da Encumeada

A sea of clouds often spill eerily over this dramatic mountain pass, from where there are views of both coasts.

P.145 ▸ THE WEST

▶ Pico Ruivo

Don't miss the chance to walk to the island's highest peak for unforgettable Alpine-like scenery.

P.168 ▸ NORTHERN MADEIRA

▼ Garajau

A statue of Christ guards these spectacular sea cliffs, just east of the capital.

P.113 ▸ THE SOUTHEAST AND
        MACHICO

Swimming

It's commonly assumed that Madeira has few beaches, but in fact nearly every coastal village has some sort of beach or jetty that you can swim off. There are fifteen blue flag beaches in total, and though most of these consist of large stones, two have soft sand. Many places also have a *complexo balnear* (lido) or coastal sea pools as well.

▲ Porto Santo

The island's southeast coast is one long expanse of superb sand, perfect for families.

P.176 ▸ PORTO SANTO

▲ Porto Moniz

This north-coast village is famed for its natural sea pools, hollowed out from the volcanic rock.

P.151 ▸ PORTO MONIZ AND THE NORTHWEST

▼ Caniço de Baixo

The clear waters here are part of a pristine marine reserve.

▲ Foz da Ribeira

Sea pools in an idyllic river valley on the dramatic north coast.

▲ Prainha

This popular stretch of soft black sand is Madeira's only natural sandy beach.

▼ Calheta

Specially imported Saharan sand has been used to create Madeira's closest equivalent to a beach resort.

Parks and gardens

Madeira means "wood" and was so named because of its lauraceous forests, one of the earth's last great concentrations of laurel trees – in 1999 they were declared a UNESCO world heritage site. The island's climate also supports a wide range of the world's most beautiful cultivated flora, many introduced from ships calling in on their way back from South Africa, Australasia, Asia and South America. As a result, many parks and gardens have exotic plants bursting into bloom virtually year round.

▲ **Jardim Botânico, Funchal**
Funchal's botanical gardens offer a diverse range of stunning flora, from palms to exotic cacti and bird-of-paradise plants.

P.87 ▶ EASTERN FUNCHAL AND THE OLD TOWN

▶ Jardim de Santa Catarina

A scenic and popular town park, complete with a lake and fine views.

▲ Jardins Tropicais do Monte

A park-cum-museum, sporting works of art, decorative tiles, koi carp and abundant tropical vegetation.

▼ Rosarium, Arco de São Jorge

Portugal's largest rose collection, with over a thousand species.

▼ Quinta do Palheiro Ferreiro

Elaborate formal gardens that show off Madeira's prolific plant life.

Museums

In its heyday, Madeira was a glorified service station on the shipping highways between Europe, Africa, South America and Asia. Christopher Columbus set up here, keen to exploit the island's rich commercial potential, as did the Flemish, who traded works of art for sugar. This exchange has left a rich legacy of artefacts and paintings that can be enjoyed in Madeira's museums.

▲ Museu de Arte Sacra

Set in a former Bishop's Palace, the Renaissance Flemish paintings here are testament to Madeira's once-powerful trading status.

P.58 ▶ CENTRAL FUNCHAL

▼ Casa Museu Cristovão Colombo

The great explorer's heavily restored Porto Santo home, full of fascinating memorabilia.

P.178 ▶ PORTO SANTO

▲ Palácio de São Lourenço

Funchal's most impressive historic building, comprising a series of magnificent state rooms stuffed with works of art.

P.54 ▶ CENTRAL FUNCHAL

▼ Madeira Story Centre

An engaging multimedia romp through the island's history.

P.85 ▶ EASTERN FUNCHAL AND THE OLD TOWN

▲ Forte de São Tiago

The capital's seventeenth-century fortress, where you can visit an eclectic collection of modern art and then clamber round the ramparts.

P.86 ▶ EASTERN FUNCHAL AND THE OLD TOWN

▶ Museu Fotografia Vicentes

An evocative collection of black-and-white photos of nineteenth- and twentieth-century Madeira.

P.59 ▶ CENTRAL FUNCHAL

Azulejos

Madeira has some fine examples of azulejos, the distinctive Portuguese glazed tiles which are used to decorate everything from the exterior of houses, walls and fountains to the interiors of churches and cafés. The craft was brought to Portugal by the Moors in the eighth century – the word "azulejo" derives from the Arabic *al-zulecha*, "small stone". Useful both for insulation and decoration, tiles continue to be used on buildings to this day, though most are now factory-produced imitations of the old hand-painted forms.

▲ Jardins Tropicais do Monte Palace

These modern azulejos illustrate key moments in Portuguese history.

P.96 ▸ MONTE AND NORTHEAST OF FUNCHAL

▲ Casa dos Azulejos

Fine Portuguese tiles alongside examples from Turkey, Syria and elsewhere.

P.60 ▸ CENTRAL FUNCHAL

▲ Convento de Santa Clara

The seventeenth-century tiles in this convent are some of the oldest on the island.

P.61 ▸ CENTRAL FUNCHAL

▶ Quinta Vigia

Azulejos depicting the life of Saint Francis embellish the chapel of the president's house.

P.69 ▸ WESTERN FUNCHAL AND THE HOTEL ZONE

▼ Avenida Arriaga

The former Chamber of Commerce on Avenida Arriaga is typical of some of central Funchal's elaborately decorated older buildings.

P.56 ▸ CENTRAL FUNCHAL

Festivals

Usually coinciding with local saints' days or harvests, Madeira's festivals are occasions for the locals to let rip, and they follow a similar format: religious services in the church followed by folk dancing, usually accompanied by live music. Food stalls, lots of alcohol and sometimes fireworks enliven the proceedings. The main festivals have become more commercial, with the biggest ones – at New Year and for carnival – now major tourist attractions.

▲ Madeira Wine Festival

Kick off your shoes and join in the grape-treading with the locals.

P.200 ▶ ESSENTIALS

▲ New Year's Eve fireworks

Welcome the New Year in with a bang, with some of the finest fireworks you'll ever see.

P.199 ▶ ESSENTIALS

▶ Classic Car Rally

The annual touring of hardy relics dating back to the 1920s.

P.200 ▸ ESSENTIALS

▼ Columbus week

Porto Santo's Columbus week celebrations involve a replica sixteenth-century sailing boat and a mock wedding.

P.200 ▸ ESSENTIALS

▼ Funchal Carnival

The closest Europe has to a Rio-style parade.

P.59 ▸ CENTRAL FUNCHAL

▲ Festa da Flor

This three-day flower festival turns central Funchal into a riot of colour.

P.200 ▸ ESSENTIALS

Children's Madeira

With its stony beaches and traditionally older visitors, Madeira has a somewhat unjustified reputation for not being suitable for children. If your children are only happy with buckets and spades on a big sandy beach, then Porto Santo is a better option. However, for older children who enjoy outdoor activities, there's no shortage of things to do at any time of the year. As on mainland Portugal, children are welcomed everywhere and, while you're unlikely to find specific facilities such as baby-changing areas, the locals will do their best to accommodate children's requirements.

▲ Horse rides, Porto Santo

Take a traditional *carriola*, a covered pony trap, to Porto Santo's superb beach.

P.193 ▸ ESSENTIALS

▼ Jungle Rain café

A remote but hugely popular family restaurant, complete with jungle noises and stuffed animals.

P.148 ▸ THE WEST

▲ The lido

A fine escape for children, with rocks to scrabble on and safe bathing pools.

P.73 ▶ WESTERN FUNCHAL AND THE HOTEL ZONE

▲ Parque Temático, Santana

Seven hectares of multimedia pavilions, rides and children's attractions.

P.166 ▶ NORTHERN MADEIRA

▶ The Madeira balloon

Get high in this tethered balloon rising above the harbour.

P.54 ▶ CENTRAL FUNCHAL

Weird and wonderful

Madeira's last eruption fizzled out 890,000 years ago, but its geological origins are still evident in its bold and occasionally weird landscape, in which former volcanic peaks are punctuated with dramatic cliffs, caves and plateaus. Portuguese settlers have added to these natural wonders with a network of *levadas*, road tunnels and monuments. The most familiar artificial wonder is probably the Santana house, still common on the north coast.

▲ Terreiro da Luta

A towering monument commemorating the end of World War I, set high on a slope above Funchal.

P.98 ▸ MONTE AND NORTHEAST OF FUNCHAL

▲ Grutas de São Vicente

Ancient lava flows have left a warren of textured underground caverns buried in the hills outside São Vicente.

P.157 ▶ PORTO MONIZ AND THE NORTHWEST

▶ Santana houses

The highly practical and picturesque Santana houses still house the odd family, though most are now used for cattle.

P.167 ▶ NORTHERN MADEIRA

▲ Paúl da Serra

Driving across these high moors through mist is an eerie experience; when the weather clears, the views are superb.

P.144 ▶ THE WEST

◀ Cabo Girão

Peer down from the top of one of the world's highest sea cliffs.

P.108 ▶ NORTHWEST OF FUNCHAL

Historic Madeira

Madeira was settled in the fifteenth century by the Portuguese; they established lucrative sugar plantations, and soon the island became a major trading post. In the early seventeenth century, the wine trade, backed by powerful British merchants, led to the emergence of a wealthy elite, who also prospered from local embroidery and basket-weaving. But the majority of the islanders lived a harsh existence until the late twentieth century, when tourism and EU funds gave the island a leg-up into the modern age.

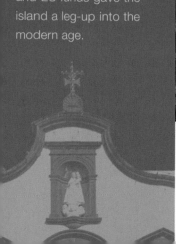

▲ Monte

An important pilgrimage spot, in the mid-1800s the cool heights of Monte also became the favoured destination for the island's first tourists.

P.93 ▸ MONTE AND NORTHEAST OF FUNCHAL

▲ Machico

The island's capital from 1440 to 1496, Machico was the first place on the island to be colonized.

P.118 ▸ THE SOUTHEAST AND MACHICO

▼ The Hotel Zone

The island's first luxury hotel, *Reid's* attracted distinguished guests such as the Churchills and blazed a trail for the plethora of modern hotels that ensure tourism remains Madeira's main source of income.

P.72 ▶ WESTERN FUNCHAL AND THE HOTEL ZONE

▲ Old Blandy's Wine Lodge

The oldest wine lodge on the island, dating back to the early seventeenth century.

P.56 ▶ CENTRAL FUNCHAL

▼ Antiga Alfândega

Located on the major shipping routes, Madeira thrived on international trade, though much of this former customs house was destroyed in the earthquake of 1748.

P.51 ▶ CENTRAL FUNCHAL

▲ Lauraceous forests

The island's ancient laurel woods, protected by UNESCO, are relics of prehistoric times.

P.166 ▶ NORTHERN MADEIRA

Unspoilt villages

To experience Madeira at its tranquil best means a visit to one of its idyllic villages, where life goes on pretty much as it always has. Hotels are gradually opening in some of these places, too, offering the chance to savour village life after the tour coaches have gone.

▲ Ponta do Sol

With its own little beach, Ponta do Sol is wedged into a valley swathed in banana plantations.

P.139 ▶ THE WEST

▼ São Vicente

Its leafy pedestrianized streets make São Vicente one of the most picturesque spots on the island.

P.156 ▶ PORTO MONIZ AND THE NORTHWEST

▶ Jardim do Mar
A tranquil village with a burgeoning surf culture, set at the foot of towering cliffs.

P.140 ▶ THE WEST

▼ Porto da Cruz
A spectacularly sited north-coast village with its own sea pools.

P.131 ▶ THE EAST AND PORTO DA CRUZ

▼ Câmara de Lobos
This earthy fishing village – Churchill's favourite – has atmosphere by the truck-load.

P.104 ▶ NORTHWEST OF FUNCHAL

Shopping

The majority of Madeira's goods have to be imported from mainland Portugal, so, not surprisingly, the best-value items are those produced locally, notably wicker, embroidery, tapestry and knitwear. Souvenirs of the edible kind include *bolo de mel* (a spiced caked made from dried fruit and molasses), jars of honey and *pastéis de nata* (Portuguese custard tarts). Madeira wine is the most popular purchase, and Funchal has several *adegas* (wine cellars) where you can sample the produce before you buy.

▲ Mercado, Santa Cruz

Rated the best on the island for fish, this market is another fine place to purchase local ingredients.

P.117 ▸ THE SOUTHEAST AND MACHICO

▼ Casa do Turista

Part museum, part shop, this place sells a whole variety of traditional produce, from ceramics to liqueurs.

P.63 ▸ CENTRAL FUNCHAL

▶ Mercado dos Lavradores

Funchal's bustling crafts, fruit, fish and vegetable market shows off the island's rich natural produce.

P.84 ▶ EASTERN FUNCHAL AND THE OLD TOWN

▼ O Relógio, Camacha

Wicker products galore are sold in this shop in the mountains above Funchal.

P.122 ▶ THE SOUTHEAST AND MACHICO

▲ Quinta da Boa Vista

Orchid plants and seedlings can be purchased here and packed and sealed for the journey home.

P.88 ▶ EASTERN FUNCHAL AND THE OLD TOWN

◀ Old Blandy's Wine Lodge

Find out how Madeira is made, then purchase the island's famous tipple.

P.56 ▶ CENTRAL FUNCHAL

Hotels

Ever since *Reid's* opened towards the end of the nineteenth century, Madeira has had a reputation for top-quality accommodation, and the majority of the island's hotels are rated four stars and over. Many are in the so-called Hotel Zone just west of central Funchal, but there are plenty of options elsewhere, too, including country houses, luxury inns, spa resorts and inexpensive guesthouses.

▲ Quinta Bela São Tiago

A perfect hideaway, with all creature comforts, in the heart of Funchal's Old Town.

P.89 ▸ EASTERN FUNCHAL AND
        THE OLD TOWN

▼ Quinta Mãe dos Homens

Affordable apartments with a pool and fabulous views over Funchal.

P.89 ▸ EASTERN FUNCHAL AND
        THE OLD TOWN

▶ CS Madeira

A touch of modern flair in Funchal, with its own spa and superb sea terrace.

P.75 ▶ WESTERN FUNCHAL AND
THE HOTEL ZONE

◀ Reid's Palace Hotel

One of the world's great hotels where tradition is the key word.

P.77 ▶ WESTERN FUNCHAL AND
THE HOTEL ZONE

▼ Luamar, Porto Santo

Great family-friendly apartments virtually on the beach.

P.185 ▶ PORTO SANTO

▶ Quinta do Arco, Arco de São Jorge

Rural self-catering at its best, near Portugal's largest rose gardens.

P.173 ▶ NORTHERN
MADEIRA

Cool Madeira

Madeira has a slightly stuffy image, reinforced by its associations with the likes of Winston Churchill and old-fashioned wines. Yet the island is far from being exclusively about crusted ports and crusty people. Its university helps promote a lively young scene, while top architects and designers have added modern flair to the island's traditional styles.

▼ Choupana Hills

Up in the hills and up there with the best of Europe's chic spa resorts.

P.102 ▸ MONTE AND NORTHEAST OF FUNCHAL

▼ Porto Santo Golf

The best of the new generation of buildings on Porto Santo, combining contemporary design and tradition.

P.181 ▸ PORTO SANTO

▼ Café do Museu

A cool watering hole for hip Funchalense.

P.66 ▸ CENTRAL FUNCHAL

▲ Estalagem da Ponta do Sol

Surreal swimming on a clifftop high above Ponta do Sol.

P.146 ▸ THE WEST

▲ Quinta da Casa Branca

Showpiece hotel surrounded by tropical vegetation.

P.76 ▸ WESTERN FUNCHAL AND THE HOTEL ZONE

▶ Casa das Mudas

A stylish clifftop arts centre showcasing big names in the art world.

P.140 ▸ THE WEST

Cafés and bars

Virtually every village in Madeira has at least one bar or café, usually open from around 8am to 10pm, sometimes later in the larger resorts. Outside Funchal, cafés often double up as the local shop. The distinction between cafés and bars is blurred; you can usually get a coffee, beer or a glass of wine in both. Even the most basic place will serve simple food such as sandwiches; the larger ones will serve full meals. In Funchal, many cafés and bars play the latest sounds, show live soccer on TV in the corner, or have karaoke or live music.

▲ **Gel Burger**

A table under the palms at *Gel Burger* is the best place to sample Porto Santo's laid-back lifestyle.

P.186 ▶ PORTO SANTO

▲ **Mercade Velho**

Machico's old market building has been tastefully converted into an appealing café.

P.123 ▶ THE SOUTHEAST AND MACHICO

▲ O Precipício

Simple café-bar with a view to die for (if you get too near the edge).

P.147 ▶ THE WEST

▶ Cervejaria Beerhouse

Funchal's marina forms a decorative backdrop to the *Cervejaria Beerhouse*'s home-brewed beer and delicious Madeiran cuisine.

P.66 ▶ CENTRAL FUNCHAL

◄ Café do Teatro

Drinks, snacks, ice creams and luvvies: the best place to be seen in Funchal.

P.67 ▶ CENTRAL FUNCHAL

Restaurants

Madeira has a good range of places to eat, from tiny backstreet cafés to upmarket restaurants facing the sea. Places geared to tourists – in particular hotel restaurants – tend to serve expensive, high-quality international cuisine. You'll find better-value and more authentic Madeiran cuisine, especially outside Funchal, at smaller restaurants such as *marisqueiras*, specializing in seafood, and *churrascarias*, which serve grills.

▲ Quinta Furão

Restaurant views don't come better than this, and the food comes a close second.

P.173 ▸ NORTHERN MADEIRA

▼ Xoupana, Choupana Hills

A slick restaurant offering fusion and eastern-inspired dining with sublime views.

P.103 ▸ MONTE AND NORTHEAST OF FUNCHAL

▲ Riso

Minimalist decor, sea views and a range of sumptuous rice dishes.

P.92 ▸ EASTERN FUNCHAL AND THE OLD TOWN

◀ Arsénio's

Sizzling grills accompanied by live fado.

P.91 ▸ EASTERN FUNCHAL AND THE OLD TOWN

▼ O Calhetas

Beachside dining on Porto Santo, with fantastic fresh fish.

P.186 ▸ PORTO SANTO

Places

Central Funchal

Dramatically sited overlooking the Atlantic, the island's capital, Funchal, sits in a natural amphitheatre surrounded by mountains: head any distance inland and you'll be climbing steeply uphill. The natural magnet for visitors is the extensive seafront, Avenida do Mar. At one end is the marina, the departure point for boat trips around the island, and buzzing with restaurants and cafés. Inland is the historic centre, a series of mosaic-paved streets lined with shops, museums and subtropical gardens, radiating out from the Sé (cathedral) and the Praça do Município, the main square.

Avenida do Mar

Funchal's main seaside drag is broad, palm-fringed Avenida do Mar, lined with kiosk cafés, most overlooking the town beach. Despite its ash-like black sand, the beach attracts bathers in summer, while at other times it's a pleasant enough place to sit and watch the crashing waves.

Opposite the central stretch of beach is the **Antiga Alfândega**, the old customs house, a relic from Funchal's days of thriving international trade and now the seat of Madeira's regional parliament. The original Renaissance building was largely destroyed in the Great Earthquake of 1748, though some features, such as a Manueline doorway at the northern end, have survived.

Also on the avenida stands a small stone column, all that remains of **Banger's Tower**, which was mostly demolished in 1939 to make way for the road. The original structure, some 30m high and nearly 3m in

▼ FUNCHAL

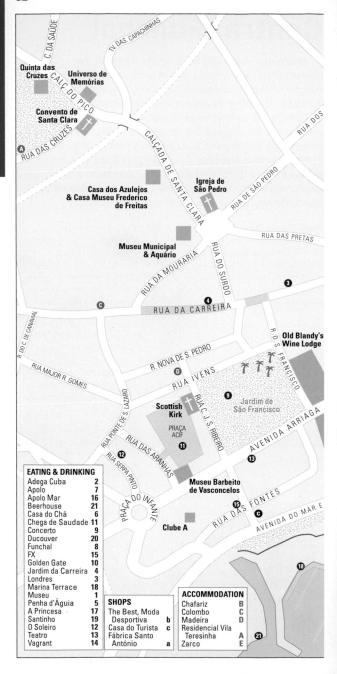

Quinta das Cruzes

Universe de Memórias

Convento de Santa Clara

RUA DAS CRUZES

C. DA SAÚDE

CALÇ. DO PICO

TV. DAS CAPACHINHAS

CALÇADA DE SANTA CLARA

RUA DOS

RUA DE SÃO PEDRO

Igreja de São Pedro

Casa dos Azulejos & Casa Museu Frederico de Freitas

RUA DAS PRETAS

Museu Municipal & Aquário

RUA DA MOURARIA

RUA DO SURDO

RUA DA CARREIRA

R. DO C. DE CANAVIAL

RUA MAJOR R. GOMES

R. NOVA DE S. PEDRO

RUA IVENS

Old Blandy's Wine Lodge

R. D. S. FRANCISCO

Jardim de São Francisco

RUA C. J. S. RIBEIRO

AVENIDA ARRIAGA

Scottish Kirk

PRAÇA ACIF

RUA PONTE DE S. LÁZARO

RUA DAS ARANHAS

RUA SERRA PINTO

Museu Barbeito de Vasconcelos

RUA DAS FONTES

PRAÇA DO INFANTE

AVENIDA DO MAR E

Clube A

EATING & DRINKING

Adega Cuba	2
Apolo	7
Apolo Mar	16
Beerhouse	21
Casa do Chá	6
Chega de Saudade	11
Concerto	9
Ducouver	20
Funchal	8
FX	15
Golden Gate	10
Jardim da Carreira	4
Londres	3
Marina Terrace	18
Museu	1
Penha d'Águia	5
A Princesa	17
Santinho	19
O Soleiro	12
Teatro	13
Vagrant	14

SHOPS

The Best, Moda Desportiva	b
Casa do Turista	c
Fábrica Santo António	a

ACCOMMODATION

Chafariz	B
Colombo	C
Madeira	D
Residencial Vila Teresinha	A
Zarco	E

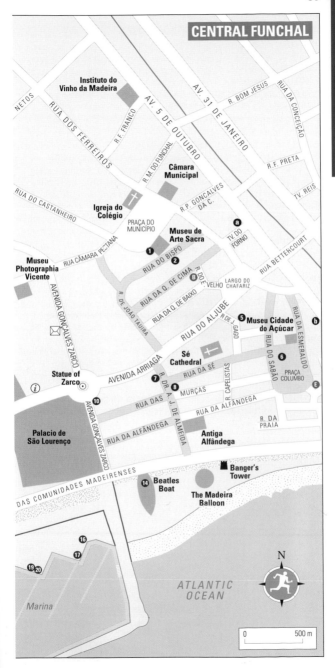

CENTRAL FUNCHAL

Central Funchal **PLACES**

diameter, was built in 1798 by a British merchant, John Banger, as a kind of crane for loading ships' cargo and later became a signpost to let market traders know what goods incoming ships were bringing in.

The Madeira Balloon

Avenida do Mar. Daily 9am–9pm every 15min. €15, children under 14 €10. A good way to get your bearings in the centre is to take a ride on the Madeira Balloon, a tethered balloon that rises high enough to give you spectacular views over the cruise ships in the harbour. Go after dark and the city is lit up around you like a magic carpet.

The marina

The attractive marina, with its sleek yachts and terraced restaurants, is one of the liveliest spots in the city, certainly after dark. When there's a big soccer game on, locals crowd the pavements outside any place with a TV; at other times, expect a hard sell from prowling waiters. This is also the place to head for boat trips, with ticket stalls lined up at the marina's eastern end.

Moored nearby is the so-called *Beatles Boat*, a luxury yacht built in the USA for the millionaire Horace Vanderbilt and owned for a time by the Beatles. Sold to a Madeiran businessman, in 1982 it was moored in its present position and turned into *The Vagrant* café-restaurant (see p.67).

Palácio de São Lourenço

Entrance on Avenida Gonçalves Zarco. Free visits on Wed at 10am,

▼ THE MARINA, FUNCHAL

Fri at 3pm & Sat at 11am; booking advisable on ☎ 291 202 530. With its distinctive white facade and single tower, the Palácio de São Lourenço is one of Funchal's most impressive and historic buildings. Today it is the official residence of the Minister of the Republic for Madeira – basically Madeira's MP in the Portuguese government. The original palace was built by the first captains of Madeira, though most of the present structure dates back to the period of Spain's brief occupation of Portugal in the sixteenth century. The east wing belongs to the army, but visitors are allowed into the Minister's state rooms in the west wing.

Highlights include the **Ballroom**, full of priceless antiques, including Louis XV mirrors and Louis XVI chairs. The Red Room houses several ornaments from the Palácio da Ajuda in Lisbon, built by Dona Maria II and Dom Ferdinand, nineteenth-century royals who had a penchant for over-the-top, generally tasteless artefacts.

The **Bulwark Room** was one of the last rooms Marcelo Caetano – the successor to the dictator Salazar (see p.206) – used

▲ PALÁCIO DE SÃO LOURENÇO

before he was exiled to Brazil following Portugal's peaceful revolution of 1974. The residents of Funchal gave him a hard time, heckling him with cat-calls during his brief stay.

Museu Barbeito de Vasconcelos

Avda Arriaga 48. Mon–Fri 10am–1pm & 3–6pm, Sat 9.30am–1.30pm. €1. The basement of Diogos Wine Shop hides one of Funchal's quirkier museums, the Museu Barbeito de Vasconcelos, the private collection of a local who had a passion both for Madeira and all things to do with Christopher Columbus. The rather rambling

Zarco

Avenida Arriaga is graced by the Monumento João Gonçalves Zarco, a statue of the discoverer of Madeira by local artist Francisco Franco. João Gonçalves gained his nickname Zarco ("one-eyed") after he lost an eye fighting the Moors while he was a knight serving Henry the Navigator during Portugal's Golden Age of global expansion in the early fifteenth century. The king decided to entrust Zarco with a mission to explore the coast off Guinea. Zarco set sail in 1418 with another captain, Tristão Vaz Teixeira, but as they headed south their boat was blown off course. They fetched up on Porto Santo, and saw a densely wooded island beyond, which they called Ilha da Madeira "island of wood". They reported back to Dom Henrique on their findings and two years later returned to make the previously uninhabited Ilha da Madeira their home. Zarco became the island's governor, settling in Funchal on the site of the current-day Quinta das Cruzes. Zarco's descendants continued to serve as governors of the island until the Spanish occupation of 1580. The navigator's remains lie buried in Funchal's Convento de Santa Clara.

collection consists of paintings, poems, opera scores and books relating mostly to Columbus's first voyage to America, and also to his time in Madeira and Porto Santo. Among the displays are a copy of the first work written on Columbus in 1576, as well as a series of portraits of the explorer dating from the seventeenth to the twentieth centuries. Unless you're particularly interested in Columbus, you'll get more out of the collection of old maps, pictures and books about Madeira itself, including *An Historical Sketch of the Island of Madeira* dating from 1819.

Jardim de São Francisco

The leafy expanse of the Jardim de São Francisco was once part of the Convento de São Francisco, and some of the convent ruins are still visible amid the jungle of frangipani, tulip trees and ferns. In the north of the park by a small lake there's a good kiosk café (see p.64), set next to a concrete amphitheatre that occasionally hosts live concerts. The neighbouring Scottish Kirk is an attractive wooden church built in 1861 which still serves the local Presbyterian community.

▼ INSIDE THE SÉ

Old Blandy's Wine Lodge

Avda Arriaga 28. Mon–Fri 9.30am–6.30pm, Sat 10am–1pm. Free. Tours Mon–Fri at 10.30am, 2.30pm, 3.30pm & 4.30pm, Sat at 11am. €4.50. Set in the Adegas de São Francisco, this is Funchal's oldest wine lodge, where you can sample and buy some of the big names in Madeira wine: Blandy, Miles, Leacock and Cossart Gordon. Parts of the building date from a sixteenth-century Franciscan monastery which stood here before the order was banned from Portugal in the nineteenth century. The present structure is mostly seventeenth century. Incorporated into the grounds is one of Funchal's oldest streets, dating back to the fifteenth century, along which casks would once have been taken to the harbour.

Though you can wander round a series of atmospheric shops and tasting rooms at will, it's worth joining one of the informative 45-minute tours, which include visits to rooms otherwise closed to the public. Among them is a series of low-ceilinged chambers where top Madeiras mature in vast wooden barrels, some as high as 3m and holding up to 9000 litres of wine. Guides explain the processes behind making the best Madeiran wines, such as the 1908 Bual, which spent 76 years ageing in a cask and costs over €500 per bottle. The tour ends back in the bar where you get the chance to sample the various wines you have seen maturing.

The Sé

Rua da Sé. Daily 8am–noon & 4.30–6.30pm. Free. Funchal's cathedral, the Sé, was built between 1485 and 1514. Its dark basalt-stone exterior and narrow windows are typical of southern

▲ MANUELINE FLOURISHES, THE SÉ

European Gothic architecture, though it also has a number of homegrown features, most notably its chequered, Hispano–Arabic style roof, carved from local wood. Around the back of the church are spiralling turrets, typical of Manueline architecture. The most striking feature inside is the geometric patterned wood and ivory ceiling, of unmistakable Moorish inspiration and somewhat at odds with the heavy Baroque decoration imposed on the rest of the interior.

Museu Cidade do Açucar

Praça Colombo 5. Mon–Fri 10am–12.30pm & 2–6pm. €2. The Museu Cidade do Açucar is devoted to the history of the island's sugar trade. Most of the collection is fairly dull and consists of sixteenth-century ceramics, religious icons, fifteenth-century sugar moulds and other items connected to the industry that launched Madeira's economy until wine took over.

Of more interest is the building, which occupies the site of what is popularly known as "Columbus's House", though it's believed that Columbus only stayed here briefly in 1498 as a guest of the owner, a sugar merchant, João Esmeraldo, before he set sail for the Americas. The original house was demolished in 1876, then excavated in 1986, revealing several important archeological finds, including the house's original well, given pride of place in the museum.

Instituto do Vinho da Madeira

Entrance on Rua 5 de Outubro. Wine museum: Mon–Fri 9am–noon & 2–6pm. Free. The towered Instituto do Vinho da Madeira was designed by eccentric British consul Henry Veitch in the nineteenth century and now houses an important institution, which declares the vintage years for all Madeira wine. The institute's **wine museum**, accessed via the central courtyard, contains a mildly interesting collection of grape-picking baskets, barrel scales and corking machines. There are, however, some wonderfully evocative black-and-white photos of the *borracheiros*, the so-called "drunken" men, whose job it was to carry the hefty goatskins of wine across the island from the farms to the capital; unsurprisingly, they drank a little of their burden to keep them going on the way.

Praça do Município

Praça do Município, the mosaic-paved main square, is one of Funchal's prettiest, with a fountain at its centre, red-flowering tulip trees in one corner and in another some fine examples of the extraordinary kapok tree, the pods of which explode into giant cottonwool balls in spring. The east side of the square is dominated by the Câmara Municipal, the town hall, built in 1758 for a local landowner, the Conde de Carvalhal. The guard will happily let you stroll into the central courtyard, beautifully lined with azulejos.

Also on the square is the Igreja do Colégio, a rather dour-looking seventeenth-century church. Inside, however, you'll find beautiful azulejos dating from the seventeenth and eighteenth centuries.

Museu de Arte Sacra

Rua do Bispo 21. Tues–Sun 10am–12.30pm & 2.30–6pm. €3. The Museu de Arte Sacra, occupying three floors of an eighteenth-century former bishop's palace, is one of the finest art galleries in Portugal, let alone Madeira, thanks to its priceless collection of Renaissance Flemish paintings. Trading links with Flanders were strong in the fifteenth and sixteenth centuries and there was a ready market for Flemish art among church and government officials and sugar-plantation owners, keen to decorate their chapels. Indeed, wealthy landowners even commissioned their own works of art from Flanders. These artworks remained unprotected and often neglected in private lodgings, chapels and churches around the island until the 1930s, when a restoration programme was undertaken in the Museu de Arte Antiga in Lisbon, and the Museu de Arte Sacra was inaugurated in 1955.

Among the most powerful works are the triptych *Descending from the Cross*, attributed to Gerard David (1518–27), and *The Annunciation*, by Joos Van Cleve (1508–45). Another valuable painting is the *Triptych of Santiago Menor and São Filipe*, by Pieter Coecke Van Aelst (1527–40). Other highlights are the sixteenth-century wooden sculpture of Christ, believed to be from the Flemish or German school; and a painting of St Jerónimo pensively fingering a skull, attributed to Marinus Van Reymerswaele (1521–40).

The rest of the collection contains Portuguese art from the sixteenth to the eighteenth centuries, while on the first floor you'll find some fine Indo–Portuguese applied arts, including stunning Indian eucharist dishes in mother-of-pearl.

▼ PRAÇA DO MUNICÍPIO

Museu Fotografia Vicentes

Rua da Carreira 43. Mon–Fri 10am–12.30pm & 2–5pm. €2.50. Entered via a superb balconied courtyard, the Museu Fotografia Vicentes marks the site of Portugal's first-ever photographic studio, set up by Vicente Gomes da Silva in 1865. As a pioneering photographer, da Silva had access to an extraordinary range of people. His clients included Empress Elizabeth of Austria and the Empress of Brazil, and he and his sons managed to photograph nearly every person of note who visited the island at the end of the nineteenth century. Photos of Churchill's visit to Câmara dos Lobos in 1950 also feature, as do shots of the first car on the island (1904) and the first regular seaplane, from Southampton (1949). Some of the most interesting of the family's collection of 380,000 images, however, are those that illustrate everyday life on the island in bygone years: bullock carts being used as public transport, sailing ships

▲ MUSEU FOTOGRAFIA VICENTES

visiting the harbour, society figures, as well as ordinary people.

Museu Municipal and Aquário

Tues–Fri 10am–6pm, Sat & Sun noon–6pm. €2.50. The Museu Municipal is mostly given over to a rather dusty and old-fashioned natural history collection, which does, however, give a fascinating insight into some of the animal life round the island. The upstairs rooms

Carnival

Carnival in Funchal (February or March) is one of Madeira's most important events of the year. Heavily influenced by Rio, with Brazilian music and risqué outfits, it is also gaining a reputation as one of the best carnivals in Europe.

The festivities kick off on the Friday with children from the local primary schools parading in fancy dress. As darkness falls local lads borrow their sisters' or mothers' garb before hitting town for "Transvestite Night".

Saturday evening is when the main parade takes place, attracting some 1500 people. At around 9pm, a procession of floats weaves down Avenida do Infant to Avenida Arriaga, before ending up on Praça do Município, the venue for the rest of the evening's music and partying. The streets around, lined with stalls selling *bolo de caco* (garlic bread) and coloured balloons, are highly atmospheric.

There's usually live music in Praça Município on Sunday and Monday, but things pep up again on Tuesday with the Great Allegorical Parade (Cortejo Trapalhão), usually processing at 4pm from the market to the Jardim de São Francisco. Anyone can wear fancy dress and coloured streamers cover the streets along the parade route. At around 6pm, there is a farewell-to-carnival show in Praça do Município, with prizes given to the best carnival costumes.

present a series of skeletons, fossils and stuffed animals native to Madeira, including huge rays, giant monk seals, whales and a crab the size of a small dog. Downstairs is a small, gloomy aquarium, containing a miserable collection of sea creatures native to Madeira's shores, including moray eels and giant snails.

Igreja de São Pedro

Rua de São Pedro. Built between the sixteenth and eighteenth centuries, the Igreja de São Pedro was the island's original cathedral and is still one of the most beautiful churches in Funchal, with an ornate Baroque altar, painted wooden ceiling and low chandeliers. Most striking are the *azulejos tapetes*, a blue and white geometric carpet of tiles on the walls dating back to the seventeenth century.

Casa dos Azulejos and Casa Museu Frederico de Freitas

Calçada de Santa Clara. Tues–Sat 10am–12.30pm & 2–5.30pm, Sun 10am–12.30pm. €2.50. The Casa dos Azulejos is a wonderful little museum containing tiles from all round the world. On the ground floor are some well-preserved examples from medieval times. Successive floors display exquisitely decorated tiles from Spain, Persia, Turkey, Holland and Syria dating from the twelfth to the nineteenth centuries; Portuguese azulejos rescued from demolished buildings on the island; and some particularly fine sixteenth-century mosaics taken from the Convento de Santa Clara.

The neighbouring Casa Museu Frederico de Freitas, occupying the attractive eighteenth-century Casa Calçada, contains miscellaneous objects collected by twentieth-century lawyer and veteran traveller, Dr Frederico de Freitas. The house has been renovated in the style of a nineteenth-century quinta (manor house). Most of the furnishings come from de Freitas's private collection and include oriental carpets, antique furniture from Britain and Portugal and religious paintings, along with collections of Chinese porcelain and Portuguese and English ceramics.

▼ CONVENTO DE SANTA CLARA

Convento de Santa Clara

Calçada de Santa Clara. Mon–Sat 10am–noon & 3–5pm. €2.50.

The atmospheric Convento de Santa Clara is a working convent, with ancient chapels and beautiful azulejos. It was founded in 1496 by Zarco's grandson, João Gonçalves de Camara, whose sister Dona Isabel was the first abbess. Most of the original convent was destroyed in a pirate attack in 1566, when the nuns fled to Curral das Freiras. The present building was constructed in the seventeenth century and still has twenty nuns in residence; if you ring the bell during visiting hours someone will show you round. Up until the nineteenth century, the order was closed, and the young girls sent here by their parents were permitted no contact at all with the outside world. You can still see the thick wooden grille between the church and the nun's private quarters, behind which the girls were confined. During the nineteenth century, conditions were relaxed slightly and the nuns were allowed to make and sell sugar sweets to visitors.

There are two cloisters – one now contains a children's playground, while the other is particularly peaceful and beautiful, filled with plants and orange trees. Adjacent to the cloisters is the church, spared in the pirate attack in 1566, lined with seventeenth century azulejos and containing the tomb of Zarco (see box on p.55).

Quinta das Cruzes

Calçada do Pico 1. Tues–Sun 10am–12.30pm & 2–5.30pm. €2.50, gardens free. The seventeenth-century estate of Quinta das Cruzes was once the private home of a Genoese wine-shipping family, the Lomelinos. Their mansion bears testimony to the wealthy lifestyle wine-merchants enjoyed on Madeira at that time, overflowing with art and silks from India and China, Flemish paintings (a highlight is Jean de Mabuse's *Three Magi),* French tapestry, English furniture and nineteenth-century jewellery. There's also a large collection of silver and china pieces, mostly dating from the eighteenth and nineteenth centuries, when the Portuguese shipped porcelain from China to Europe on a large scale. Many of the pieces were made to order and decorated with family coats of arms, or biblical and mythological themes.

Outside, the estate's garden is a verdant array of flowers and dragon trees interspersed with a somewhat esoteric gathering of tombstones, statues and stone window frames that have been rescued from various demolished buildings throughout the island. Some of these are remnants of Zarco's house, which stood on this site before the current quinta was built. Concerts are held in the gardens in summer.

Universo de Memórias

Calçada do Pico. Tues–Sat 10am–noon & 2–5pm, Sun 10am–noon. €3. Set in a superb nineteenth-century town house, the Universo de Memórias museum houses the eclectic belongings of obsessive collector João Carlos Abreu, the Madeiran minister for tourism and former journalist and travel agent. His extensive travels are evident, with many pieces from the Middle East and Orient.

Not all of the stuff is valuable and some is downright tacky, but the range is astonishing: modern surrealist art, fifteenth-century porcelain, masks, jewellery, vases, paintings, even Abreu's mum's hats and his own substantial array of ties. Upstairs there's an entire floor dedicated to his collection of horses, from funfair models to Victorian rocking horses and Murano crystal stallions. Much of the appeal of the place is the house itself, whose original features include stained-glass windows and wooden floors. There's also a tea room in the small gardens at the back.

Fortaleza do Pico

Rua do Castelo. Mon–Fri 9am–6pm. Free. Bus #15A from Praça da Autonomia. It's well worth climbing the very steep hill to Fortaleza do Pico – a ten-minute walk from the Universo de Memórias – for the stunning views back over the city. The fort was built in 1611 when Madeira was under Spanish rule and is now used by the navy; the only part open to the public is a room showing prints of the building over the years, though you are free to wander round the front ramparts and enjoy the views.

Hotels

Residencial Chafariz

Rua do Estanco Velho 3–5 ☏ 291 232 260, ⓦ freewebs.com/chafariz. Central and quiet, on a narrow pedestrianized street opposite the Sé. The good-sized rooms come complete with cable TV and en-suite bathrooms, and the fourth-floor breakfast room has great views over the town. €45.

Residencial Colombo

Rua do Carreira 182 ☏ 291 225 231/2, ⓦ www.residencias-colombo.pt. A modern, ungainly-looking guesthouse at the west end of Rua do Carreira, but rooms are good value, with phones, TV and private bathroom, and there's also a sunny roof terrace. The upper-floor rooms have views over the sea. €45.

Hotel Madeira

Rua Ivens 21 ☏ 291 230 071, ⓦ www.hotelmadeira.com. A white, modern three-star with

▼ FORTALEZA DO PICO

▲ TAXIS, AVENIDA ARRIAGA, FUNCHAL

red-faced, angled balconies in an attractive position near the Jardim de São Francisco. The rooms are small but well equipped and include satellite TV, while elsewhere there's a bar, a billiard lounge and a small rooftop pool. Pretty good value for such a central location. €70.

Residencial Vila Teresinha
Rua das Cruzes 21 ☎291 741 723, ⓦwww.vilateresinha.com. Friendly guesthouse a hefty ten-minute walk uphill from the centre, but close to many of the museums. There's a range of rooms of different sizes, the best with balconies and fine city views (€15 extra). A lovely communal terrace and decent downstairs restaurant add to the appeal. €45.

Residencial Zarco
Rua da Alfândega 113 ☎291 223 716, ⓦresidencialzarco.com. A large, family-run *residencial* with slightly shabby rooms, each with its own shower and TV. Rooms (€30) at the front can be noisy, but the position just by the seafront can't be faulted.

It also lets out apartments with kitchenettes at a nearby annexe for €35.

Shops

The Best, Moda Desportiva
Rua 5 Outubro 16–17. Mon–Fri 9am–7.30pm, Sat 9am–1pm. This small sports shop is the perfect place to stock up on walking gear before hitting the *levadas*, with a range of good-quality walking boots and sticks.

Casa do Turista
Rua do Conselheiro José Silvestre Ribeiro 2. Mon–Fri 9.30am–1pm & 2.30–6.30pm, Sat 9.30am–1pm. Part museum, part handicrafts shop, set inside the former home of the German consul. The nineteenth-century decor is impressive, though the "traditional" produce on offer – ceramics, embroidery, bags, wicker, dolls, silver, quilts, tiles, maps, guides, Madeira wine and liqueurs – is of very mixed quality. There's a small terrace at the back with a mock post office-cum-bar front and a traditional bedroom, perhaps the best part.

Fábrica Santo António

Travessa do Forno 27–29. Mon–Fri 9am–1pm & 2–7pm, Sat 9am–1pm. A traditional bakery piled high with home-made cakes, biscuits and preserves.

Cafés

Apolo Mar

Marina de Funchal. Daily 7am–1am. At the eastern end of the marina, this local café serves grilled fish and meat dishes, though most people just pop in for a drink or snack. There's a TV above the bar and shaded outdoor tables facing the bobbing boats in the marina.

Casa do Chá

Praça Columbo 35. Mon–Fri 10am–8pm, Sat 10am–2am. Attractive tea house with outside seating on this broad square, fine home-made cakes and scones, plus various Rooibos and herbal teas and coffee.

Café Concerto

Jardim de São Francisco. Daily 8am–11pm. Small kiosk with outdoor seating in the leafy municipal gardens next to the park auditorium. Offerings include full lunches, *poncha* (brandy cocktails) and wine, as well as milkshakes, sandwiches, pastries and fresh fruit juices, including kiwi, mango and papaya.

Café Funchal

Rua Dr José António Almeida. Daily 8am–midnight. One of a cluster of high-profile cafés on this pedestrianized street, this is a great spot to watch the world go by, with a counter full of cakes, and shaded outdoor seating under a blue canopy.

Pastelaria Penha d'Águia

Rua de João Gago 6–8. Mon–Fri 8am–7pm, Sat 8am–1.30pm. One of the best places in central Funchal for pastries, with a few outdoor tables facing the Sé and a long stand-up counter groaning with *pastéis de nata*, cakes, big croissants, *queijada* cheese biscuits, mini pizzas, sandwiches and *sonhos* ("dreams") – small

▼ CENTRAL FLOWER SCHOOL

round cakes dipped in dark honey.

Restaurants

Adega Cuba

Rua do Bispo 28 ☎291 220 986. Daily 8am–9pm. Opposite the Museu de Arte Sacra, this characterful *adega* (wine cellar) has a long drinks list and serves good-value lunches in a barn-like interior divided into barrel-shaped cubicles.

Apolo

Rua Dr J. António Almeida 21 ☎291 220 099. Daily 8am–11pm. A high-profile restaurant and café on a pedestrianized street linking the Sé with the seafront. The extensive menu is surprisingly reasonable with a long list of starters and good fish and meat main courses, while the house salads make an excellent light lunch.

Ducouver

Marina de Funchal ☎291 237 050. Daily 10am–1am. The aggressive marketeering to lure you in can be offputting, but the terrace affords great views over the marina and the food and service is good, with decent pasta, pizza and superb fresh fish. Other specialities include *bife na pedra* (steak cooked on a hot stone) and *peixe assado no sal* (fish baked in salt). Around €25 for a full meal.

Jardim da Carreira

Rua da Carreira 118 ☎291 222 498. Daily 10am–11pm. Popular with tourists thanks to a superb, tranquil courtyard full of flowers and trees, and with a menu featuring Madeiran staples such as tomato and onion soup with egg, and

espadarte (scabbard fish) with banana, as well as good-value set lunches. Mains €7–9.

Londres

Rua da Carreira 64a ☎291 235 329. Mon–Sat 11.30am–4pm & 6pm–midnight. A traditional restaurant with uninspiring decor but very good food, including daily specials, *bacalhau* and other fish dishes (usually sea bream, salmon and trout), along with steaks. Main from around €9.

Marina Terrace

Marina de Funchal ☎291 230 547. Daily 10am–11pm. With lots of tables on a semi-covered terrace at the west end of the marina, this is probably the best value of the larger restaurants in the area, offering simple and effective dishes such as chicken and beef kebabs, tuna cooked in wine and garlic and enormous *arroz de mariscos*, plus inexpensive house wine. Mains around €12.

A Princesa

Marina de Funchal ☎291 237 719. Daily 10am–midnight. Avoids the hard sell of the other restaurants along this stretch, perhaps because it can rely on the knowledge that its deliciously chargrilled fresh fish will pull punters back. Don't be put off by something called BSE on the wine list – it's actually rather good. Bargain set lunches start at around €10, otherwise mains start from around €9.

O Soleiro

Rua Serpa Pinto 28 ☎291 229 634. Daily noon–3pm & 6–11pm. *O Soleiro* does very good-value tuna steaks with fried maize and other dishes, along with fine house wines. If you don't fancy a full meal, you can perch at the lively bar with the locals, who crowd in when live football is on TV. Mains around €9.

Bars

Cervejaria Beerhouse

Porto de Funchal ☎291 229 011. Daily 10am–midnight. Just above the marina and sporting a distinctive, tent-like roof, this bar-restaurant brews its own fine hoppy, unfiltered beer and has superb views of Funchal, with seating inside or out. It also does fine food, including seafood with *açorda* (bread sauce), lobster and superb tuna.

Chega de Saudade

Praça da ACIF ☎291 242 289. Tues 10am–8pm, Wed–Fri 8am–midnight, Sat 6pm–3am. Fashionable, jazzy café-bar-restaurant. The international food is overpriced, but it's a nice spot for a drink on its comfy sofas or on the upstairs terrace. Live music on Saturdays, usually jazz or chillout sounds.

FX

Largo das Fontes 39 ☎965 077 875. Daily 6pm–2am. One of Funchal's trendier places, with a sleek, wood floor, a long bar and an outdoor terrace. Attracts a young clientele, expecially when there's a live band (usually at weekends), but doesn't get going till late.

Golden Gate

Avenida Arriaga 27–29 ☎291 234 383. Mon–Wed & Sun 8am–midnight, Thurs–Sat 8am–2am. This has been a fashionable meeting place since the nineteenth century, when it was a hotel bar, and it now serves everything from morning coffee and croissant to ice creams, alcohol and full meals. The decor retains a period feel, with lots of mirrors, ceiling fans and wicker chairs, and there's also a first-floor balcony and a few outside tables. At weekends the mood changes after midnight with visiting DJs and dance sounds.

Café do Museu

Praça Municipio ☎291 281 121. Mon–Sat 10am–4am. One of Funchal's

▼ CAFÉ DO MUSEU

hippest hangouts, set under the arcades of the Museu de Arte Sacra and attracting a young, arty crowd. There's an inventive drinks menu, including vodka sherbet, imaginative and good-value international food (served until 8pm), plus gentle jazzy and contemporary sounds inside, and tables facing the square outside.

Santinho

Marina do Funchal ☎ 291 228 945. Daily 10am–4am. A lively marina-side music bar, with sports TV, live music most weekends and a young crowd downing *poncha*, sangria and *caipirinhas* (Brazilian cocktails). It also does very good-value meals, including a filling *prego no bolo do caco* (beef in garlic bread).

Café do Teatro

Avenida Arriaga ☎ 291 226 371, ⓦ www.cafedoteatro.com. Mon–Thurs & Sun 8am–2am, Fri–Sat 8am–4am. Fashionable café-bar in a corner of the town theatre, with shaded outdoor tables. Meals are served until 10pm and there's often live music on Fridays. It's a good place to people-watch, and is one of the few gay-friendly bars in town.

The Vagrant

Avenida do Mar ☎ 291 223 572. Daily 11am–11pm. Also known as the *Beatles Boat* (see p.54), although it's hard to know what John, Paul and co would make of the yacht's current incarnation as an unashamedly touristy restaurant-café-bar. The tables out on deck overlooking the beach are the best, though you can also sit in one of numerous mini-boats set in shallow water and "enjoy eating with the sensation of navigating", as the publicity promises. The food itself – Portuguese dishes as well as pizza, pasta and snacks – is very average, though it's a fine place for a drink, and kids love it.

Clubs

Clube A

Marina Shopping, Avenida Arriaga ☎ 291 281 282. Fri–Sat 10pm–4am. One of the friendlier and more attractive clubs in Funchal, tastefully decorated with laminate flooring and chrome light fittings, and with an eclectic mix of old and new music. Attracts a mainly young crowd, and bar prices are reasonable.

Western Funchal and the Hotel Zone

Western Funchal consists largely of the Zona Hoteleira, or Hotel Zone, the area where most visitors to Funchal stay. This is an unashamedly upmarket holiday suburb sprawling along the busy coastal Estrada Monumental, a medley of restaurants, shops and state-of-the-art hotel complexes vying for ocean views. The area's main highlight is the leafy Jardim de Santa Catarina, the city's largest park, while other attractions include the Barbeito wine lodge; the attractive gardens of Quinta Magnolia; and the venerable Reid's, one of the world's best-known hotels. Further west sit two enormous lidos and Funchal's main beach, at Praia Formosa.

Jardim de Santa Catarina

Set on a high bluff overlooking the harbour is the city's main park, the Jardim de Santa Catarina, a wonderful swathe of breezy parkland laid out between 1945 and 1966. By the main entrance you'll see a small statue of Christopher Columbus and the Capela de Santa Catarina, an attractive (but usually locked) seventeenth-century chapel which occupies the site of an old wooden church commissioned in 1425 by the wife of Zarco. An expanse of coarse grass above this makes a good picnic spot, with superb views back over the city.

A network of paths leads uphill past giant succulents and red-flowering tulip trees. At the top end of the park, a fenced-off area next to two rusting old traction engines

▲ JARDIM DE SANTA CATARINA

▲ AZULEJOS, QUINTA VIGIA

marks a fine children's playground, just above a small lake and a park café, *Esplanade O Lago* (see p.77). Opposite the lake, across the Avenida do Infante, luxuriant foliage continues around the **Hospício da Princesa**, founded in 1859 by the empress of Brazil in memory of her daughter, Princess Maria Amélia, who died of TB in 1853 at the age of 22. Its luxuriant gardens, full of spiny dragon trees and towering palms, are open to the public.

Quinta Vigia

Avenida do Infante. Mon–Sat 9am–5pm. Free. The pink eighteenth-century Quinta Vigia, an attractive but surprisingly modest building, is the official residence of Madeira's president. Formerly the Quinta Angústias, home of the empress of Brazil during the 1850s, it stepped in to fill the shoes of the original Quinta Vigia, controversially demolished to make way for the neighbouring *Carlton Park Hotel* in the 1960s. Visitors are only allowed to visit the beautiful eighteenth-century chapel, lined with superb azulejos depicting the life of Saint Francis, and the attractive gardens, which contain peacocks, a parrot enclosure and sweeping views over the harbour.

The harbour and Loo Rock

Offering some of the best views of the city, the harbour is a bustling area of colourful fishing boats and giant cruise ships which dock early morning most days, especially around Easter. It's also the departure point for the daily ferry to Porto Santo. Surveying all is the fortress on top of Loo Rock, which juts out into the harbour. The rock was where Madeira's settlers spent their first night, feeling more secure here than on the mainland. In 1656, a small fortress was built on the rock, and a chapel to Nossa Senhora da Conceicão was

▼ FUNCHAL HARBOUR

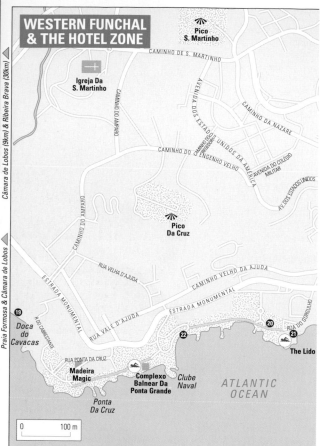

WESTERN FUNCHAL & THE HOTEL ZONE

Pico S. Martinho

CAMINHO DE S. MARTINHO

Igreja Da S. Martinho

AVENIDA DOS ESTADOS UNIDOS DA AMÉRICA

CAMINHO DA NAZARE

CAMINHO DO AMPARO

CAMINHO DO ENGENHO VELHO

AVENIDA DO COLÉGIO MILITAR

AV. DOS ESTADOS UNIDOS

Câmara de Lobos (9km) & Ribeira Brava (30km)

Pico Da Cruz

CAMINHO DO AMPARO

RUA VELHA D'AJUDA

CAMINHO VELHO DA AJUDA

ESTRADA MONUMENTAL

RUA VALE D'AJUDA

ESTRADA MONUMENTAL

RUA DO GORGULHO

Praia Formosa & Câmara de Lobos

19 Doca do Cavacas

RUA DO CABRESTANTE

RUA PONTA DA CRUZ

22

20

21 The Lido

Madeira Magic

Complexo Balnear Da Ponta Grande

Clube Naval

ATLANTIC OCEAN

Ponta Da Cruz

0   100 m

▲ LOO ROCK

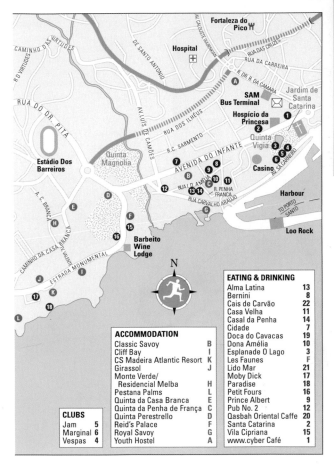

ACCOMMODATION

Classic Savoy	B
Cliff Bay	I
CS Madeira Atlantic Resort	K
Girassol	J
Monte Verde/ Residencial Melba	H
Pestana Palms	L
Quinta da Casa Branca	E
Quinta da Penha de França	C
Quinta Perestrello	D
Reid's Palace	F
Royal Savoy	G
Youth Hostel	A

CLUBS

Jam	5
Marginal	6
Vespas	4

EATING & DRINKING

Alma Latina	13
Bernini	8
Cais de Carvão	22
Casa Velha	11
Casal da Penha	14
Cidade	7
Doca do Cavacas	19
Dona Amélia	10
Esplanade O Lago	3
Les Faunes	F
Lido Mar	21
Moby Dick	17
Paradise	18
Petit Fours	16
Prince Albert	9
Pub No. 2	12
Qasbah Oriental Caffe	20
Santa Catarina	2
Vila Cipriana	15
www.cyber Café	1

added in 1682. Between 1757 and 1762, the rock was joined to the mainland, the harbour wall was gradually extended and, in 1866, a lighthouse was added. In 1992, the rock passed from the military to the local council, and the fort now houses a café-restaurant (currently closed for renovation).

Quinta Magnolia

Rua Dr Pita. Daily: May–Sept 8am–9pm; Oct–April 8am–7pm. City bus #5, #6, #8 or #45 from opposite the Marina. Pay at the main gate for sports facilities. Set in an attractive park and formerly the site of the British Country Club, the Quinta Magnolia leisure complex is an oasis of tranquillity in a busy part of the city, and a great resource if you're staying somewhere without a pool or gardens. Facilities include a children's playground, tennis courts and a large freshwater swimming pool, plus an attractive café-bar.

▲ QUINTA MAGNOLIA

Reid's Palace Hotel

Estrada Monumental 139. Bus #1,
2, 6, 24 or 35 from Avenida do Mar.
Reid's is one of the world's most
famous hotels. Though a night
– or even a meal at one of its
many restaurants – is beyond
many people's means, you can
enjoy the terrace views by
taking afternoon tea (3–5.30pm
daily; €27); you'll need to book
a day in advance on ☏291 717
171.

The hotel was founded by
William Reid, the son of
a Scottish crofter, born in
Kilmarnock in 1822. William, a
sickly child, was advised to go
to warmer climes to improve
his health. In 1836, he earned
his passage on a ship to Funchal,
where he got a job first as a
baker and later in the wine
trade. A natural entrepreneur, he
soon set up an agency catering
to wealthy tourists who wanted
to stay in local quintas, in those
days the only places to stay in
comfort. Spotting a potential
market, Reid saved enough to
buy his own place, the Quinta
das Fontes, and converted it
into a hotel. The venture had
a powerful backer, the Duke
of Edinburgh, and the hotel
was appropriately renamed the
Royal Edinburgh Hotel. Reid
soon acquired further hotels and
guesthouses, but his ambition
was to own a purpose-built
establishment, and eventually
he managed to buy Salto do
Cavalo, a five-acre estate on a
clifftop, 50m above sea level.
Sadly, Reid died three years
before his dream was realized
and the hotel was completed
in 1891, designed by George
Somers, architect of the
Shepherd's Hotel in Cairo.

In the early twentieth century,
guests arrived at the hotel's
grand sea-facing entrance by
boat or seaplane. Nowadays,
guests slip into the former staff
entrance by car. The list of
past guests reads like a who's

Madeira wine

In around 1687, a barrel of wine was left forgotten in a corner of a ship for two
long sea journeys. When a sailor was allowed to drink the "spoiled" wine, it was
discovered that the slow warming of the barrel as the ship passed to and from the
tropics had helped mature the wine. These days, this warming effect is re-created
in large vats called *estufas*, where wines are kept at temperatures of 40–50°C
for three to six months, giving the wines a slightly smoky taste. The wine is then
stored for eighteen months before it is transferred into American oak barrels. These
barrels are not tightly sealed as air actually improves the Madeira.

Madeira remains unique in its ability to improve with age, even after it has been
opened. Some islanders are said to buy a good Madeiran wine and have a glass
of it once a year to celebrate special occasions such as wedding anniversaries,
with no noticeable spoiling.

who of the last century and includes Captain Scott of the Antarctic; Edward VIII; Lloyd George; Churchill (see box on p.106); George Bernard Shaw who met resident tango instructor Max Rinder and called him "the only man that ever taught me anything"; pioneer flyer Amy Johnson; General Batista of Cuba, fleeing from Castro's revolution in 1958; Gregory Peck and John Huston, who stayed here while shooting the whale-hunting scenes in the 1956 film of *Moby Dick*; Portugal's dictator Salazar; actor Roger Moore; novelist Frederick Forsyth; and countless heads of state and European royals.

Barbeito Wine Lodge

Estrada Monumental ☎ 291 761 829. Mon–Fri 9am–12.30pm & 2–5.30pm. Bus #1, 2, 6, 24 or 35 from Avenida do Mar. Tucked away amid some of Funchal's flashest hotels lies this humble low-rise building, home to a very traditional wine producer. Stick your head in the door and you'll be overwhelmed by the warm and heady smell of Madeira wine, and be confronted by giant wine barrels and rattling bottling machines. There's a small tasting room and shop to one side, where you can sample and buy the produce.

The lido

Rua Gorgulho. Daily 8.30am–7pm. €3. City bus #6 from Avenida do Mar. The Olympic-sized seawater pool in Funchal's municipal lido is a great place to head for a proper swim. When the sea is rough, the waves literally break into the pool; in calm weather you can also climb down ladders to the rocks below and swim in the Atlantic, here part of the protected Eco-Parque Marinha do Funchal. There are other smaller pools, children's pools, along with water slides and stepping stones. Built into the cliff face above are cafés, restaurants and shops. It gets pretty packed at weekends, but otherwise makes a fine spot to laze away an afternoon.

Complexo Balnear da Ponta Grande

Daily: May–Sept 8.30am–8pm; Oct–April 8.30am–7pm. €3. Bus #1, 2 or 24 from Avenida do Mar. On the

▲ WESTERN FUNCHAL

seafront, some fifteen minutes' walk west of the main lido is another modern lido complex on a broad, flat stretch of coast, comprising sea pools, slides and sunbathing areas; there's also sea access, a café and restaurant.

Madeira Magic

Rua Ponta da Cruz 25 ☎291 700 700 ⓦwww.madeira-magic.com. Tues–Fri 10am–6pm, Sat & Sun 10am–7pm. €6, children under 17 €3.50, family ticket €15. Bus #1, #2 or #24 from Avenida do Mar. Set in sea-facing parkland, Madeira Magic is an educational resource centre and theme park which is also open to casual visitors. Families in particular will enjoy the small planetarium and the "Living Science" area, with various computer games and interactive displays. There's also a decent café-restaurant. Look on the website for details of temporary exhibits.

Praia Formosa

City bus #35 from Avenida do Mar. Beyond Praia Ponta Gordo, the seafront promenade continues west for another 1km or so to Praia Formosa, which is reached via a tunnel blasted through the rock – halfway along it, a rock window looks into a sea cave. The *praia* itself is the closest proper beach to Funchal, a long expanse of stony shore dotted with palm-frond sunshades. In 1566, it was the landing stage for Bertrand de Montluc, a French pirate, whose band of men went on to ransack Funchal. These days the beach doesn't win any beauty prizes, but has a refreshingly local feel to it, especially the western end, where there's a stretch of fine black sand, a summer go-cart track, watersports facilities and children's playground. The centrepiece of the development behind the beach will be a new stadium for Marítimo football club, due to be completed in 2008-2009.

Hotels

Hotel Classic Savoy

Avenida do Infante ☎291 213 000, ⓦwww.savoyresort.com. One

▼ PROMENADE NEAR PRAIA FORMOSA

of Funchal's older hotels: the communal areas have a nice period feel and there are three restaurants, but some of the rooms are looking their age, and none comes cheap, not even the unexceptional ones with "mountain view" – actually overlooking the hotel car park. Having said that, the tariffs do cover a vast range of facilities, including inside and outside pools, a garden with golf-driving nets, a giant chess set and a playground, plus a gym and beauty treatment room. Disabled access. €220, sea view €260.

The Cliff Bay

Estrada Monumental 147 ☏ 291 707 700, ⓦ www.cliffbay.com. This stylish, modern hotel is built into a series of terraces spilling down the cliffs. Rooms are plush, with large balconies, and the fluffy dressing gowns are to die for. It's a great place for families; facilities include indoor and outdoor pools, gym, kindergarten, four restaurants and two bars. Tennis, windsurfing, massages and fishing trips can be arranged, and there's disabled access. €410.

CS Madeira Atlantic Resort

Estrada Monumental 175–177 ☏ 291 717 700, ⓦ www .csmadeiraatlanticresort.com. It's hard to miss the concrete-and-glass exterior of this modern hotel, and the facilities here are on a par with any luxury hotel on the island. There are superb views from the minimalist rooms, all of which have balconies facing the enormous sea terrace – the largest on the island, complete with pools, a bar and glass lifts. Elsewhere you'll find squash and tennis courts, a diving centre, kids' club

and a giant thelassotherapy spa, not to mention restaurants and a cool cocktail bar. Disabled access. €160.

Hotel Girassol

Estrada Monumental 256 ☏ 291 701 570, ⓦ www.maisturismo.pt/girasol. Popular with package-tour operators, this unpromising L-shaped concrete block sits on the wrong side of the Estrada Monumental, with its sea views partially obscured by the *Crowne Plaza* opposite. Nevertheless, the good-sized rooms and suites can't be faulted, and there are two pools, a bar, restaurant, cable TV, babysitting, a games room, sauna and gym. €140.

Estalagem Monte Verde/ Residencial Melba

Azinhaga Casa Branca 8 ☏ 291 774 072, ⓔ esmonever@hotmail.com. A very good-value, low-rise hotel, five minutes' walk uphill from the Hotel Zone. The spacious rooms all have cable TV and balconies, some facing the sea, and there's a small pool at the side. Even cheaper rooms are available in a neighbouring annexe, called the *Residencial Melba*. Guests here can use the pool, making it the best-value place in the Hotel Zone. €38, sea view €40, *Residencial Melba* €30.

Pestana Palms

Rua do Gorgulho 17 ☏ 291 709 200, ⓦ www.pestana.com. Set in the lovely grounds of an old quinta, a stone's throw from the main lido. The quinta itself is now a library, and the hotel rooms are housed in a stylish modern block on the clifftop, with plush furnishings, kitchenettes and balconies with fantastic sea views. There's also a restaurant, health club, an outdoor pool and private access to the sea. €216.

Quinta da Casa Branca

Rua da Casa Branca 7 ☎ 291 700 770, ⓦ www.quintacasabranca.pt. Designed by highly rated local architect João Favila, this place has a chic, boutiquey feel. It's situated in a tranquil part of town behind a historic family quinta (still privately occupied), and has substantial grounds full of tropical foliage. Each well-equipped ground-floor room opens onto its own lawnside terrace, while rooms in the modern annexe have neat sliding shutters giving onto large balconies. There's also a health centre, pools and a separate restaurant serving gourmet Portuguese food. €185.

Quinta da Penha de França

Rua Imperatriz Dona Amélia 87 ☎ 291 204 650, ⓦ www.hotel quintapenhafranca.com. This

▼ TEA AT REID'S PLACE HOTEL

lovely old quinta is squeezed in among larger hotels just above the harbour. There's a mixed bag of good-value rooms, from the small but cosy ones with shower in the original building (from €58) to the smarter, larger ones in the modern extension, sporting balconies overlooking the small garden and pool (€105). There are more rooms at a seaside annexe by the harbour, complete with terrace-balconies (€115).

Quinta Perestrello

Rua do Dr Pita 3 ☎ 291 706 700, ⓦ www.charminghotelsmadeira.com. Dating back to the 1800s and set in small grounds, *Quinta Perestrello* has its own pool, restaurant and terrace café. Rooms are airy and wood-floored, with those in the modern extension (€17 extra) having their own terraces. The only disadvantage is its position wedged in by a busy road junction. €138.

Reid's Palace Hotel

Estrada Monumental 139 ☎ 291 717 171, ⓦ www .reidspalace.com. Madeira's first and most famous hotel (see p.72). Much of its appeal lies in its rambling size, which manages to absorb any number of visitors without ever seeming full. Recently renovated, it retains a quaint colonial air, while its subtropical gardens are full of quiet corners and tranquil viewpoints. Its array of facilities includes three restaurants, pools and sea access, a café (see p.72), various spa treatments, tranquil gardens with sweeping

▲ ESPLANADE O LAGO, JARDIM DE SANTA CATARINA

sea views and an entertainments programme, including special "Fun at Reid's" days for children. Some guests return every year, and it's easy to see why. €385.

Royal Savoy

Rua Carvalho Araújo ☎ 291 213 500, ⓦ www.savoyresort.com. One of Funchal's swishest hotels, with 162 enormous suites and large studios, each with kitchenette and sea-facing balcony. These are ranged around a lower seafront area replete with palm trees and a series of pools, while facilities also include a spa, tennis courts and restaurants. €350.

Youth Hostel

Quinta da Ribeira, Avenida Calouste Gulbenkian, Calçada da Cabouqueira 5 ☎ 291 741 540, ⓦ www.ijm.pt. Set back off a busy road – and so can be noisy – most of this hostel occupies a lovely nineteenth-century building with low stone arched ceilings, while the remainder occupies a modern extension. There are beds in airy dorms from €12.50, plus simple en-suite doubles from €21, as well as a common room, kitchen facilities and Internet access.

Cafés

Bar Santa Catarina

Avenida do Infante 22. Daily 8am–midnight. Unpromisingly positioned on a busy road at the foot of a modern shopping centre opposite Quinta Vigia, but this café does a mean range of pastries and superb *batidas* (fruit shakes), including pineapple, mango and custard apple.

Esplanade O Lago

Jardim de Santa Catarina. Daily: May–Oct 10am–9pm; Nov–April 10am–8pm. A tranquil spot by the park lake and next to the children's play area, where you can enjoy coffees, ice creams or pastries surrounded by palms, bamboos and flowering trees.

Petit Fours

Estrada Monumental 188, Loja 4. Daily 8am–8pm. A modern café offering great croissants, fresh bread and pastries, with a few tables set out on a patio inside the neighbouring shopping centre.

Restaurants

Bernini

Rua Imperatriz D. Amélia 68 ☎291 230 323. Daily noon–3pm & 6.30–10.30pm. Just below the casino complex, this unpretentious glass-fronted Italian restaurant offers a long list of home-made pasta dishes, pizza, salads and Portuguese staples, not to mention a fine passionfruit liqueur. A friendly place, and popular with families. Mains from €9.

Casa Velha

Rua Imperatriz D. Amélia 69 ☎291 205 600. Daily 12.30–3pm & 7–11pm. The most atmospheric of the restaurants in the little triangle of traditional buildings behind

▼ DOCA DO CAVACAS

the casino complex, the *Casa Velha* has a semi-tropical, colonial feel, occupying a nineteenth-century villa with ceiling fans, old prints on the walls and a luxuriant garden. It's usually bustling and not too formal, serving fish, meat and superb desserts, including crepes and banana flambés. Mains around €12–15.

Doca do Cavacas

Estrada Monumental ☎291 762 052. Daily noon–10.30pm. This lovely traditional whitewashed building perches over the sea on the promenade, offering fresh and moderately priced fish and (a few) meat dishes. Or just pop into the bar opposite, hewn into the volcanic rock.

Dona Amélia

Rua Imperatriz D. Amélia 83 ☎291 225 784. Daily 12.30–3pm & 7–11pm. Set in an attractive, traditional building lined with hanging plants and azulejos. The meat dishes are hit or miss, but the seafood and pasta are usually good and reasonably priced, as are the speciality flambés. Desserts include *kebab de frutos tropicais*. There's also a basement bar. Mains from around €13.

Lido Mar

Rua do Gorgulho-Lido ☎291 764 369. Daily noon–3pm & 6–11pm. This lido restaurant is set in an attractive spot overlooking the sea and the pools below – you can eat in even if you're not using the lido facilities. The long menu offers a wide range of well-prepared dishes from around €15, including tangy *arroz de tamboril* (monkfish rice) and *bacalhau*.

Moby Dick
Estrada Monumental 187 ☎ 291 776 868. Mon–Sat 11am–midnight. This place is much better than its location in the dull forecourt of a modern block would suggest. The interior is pleasantly traditional, while specialities include excellent seafood dishes such as *gambas piri piri* (spicy prawns), a few vegetarian options and what some people consider to be the best fresh fish in Funchal. The owner will pick up customers from their hotel in his minibus (minimum of four people). Fresh fish dishes starts at €11.

Paradise
Estrada Monumental 179 ☎ 291 762 559. Daily 10am–midnight. In an idyllic position facing the sea, with its own seawater swimming pools on a sun terrace below the cliffs. Service is swift and the Madeiran and Portuguese cuisine is good and well priced. Dishes include *leitão* (roast suckling pig), *pato* (duck) and the usual fish dishes.

Qasbah Oriental Caffé
Passeio Público Marítimo ☎ 291 765 500. Mon–Fri 11am–midnight, Sat & Sun 10am–midnight; daily until 2am in July and August. Along the promenade west of the Lido, this bright restaurant with outdoor decking serves excellent Middle-Eastern inspired cuisine, including *tajines*, tuna steak with couscous and pumpkin with ginger soup. Special nights include belly dancing on Wednesdays, plus occasional live music at weekends. Mains around €12, or you can just pop in for a drink.

Vila Cipriana
Estrada Monumental 139 ☎ 291 717 171. Daily 7–10.30pm. The island's best Italian restaurant, with sparkling views plus first-rate service and food, including superb antipasti, delectable pasta, sublime risottos and mouthwatering desserts such as chocolate cake with berry compote. Mains from €30; reservations advised.

Bars

Alma Latina
Rua Imperatriz Dona Amélia 101. Mon–Sat noon–2am. Sophisticated modern bar with wooden floors and subtle lighting. It gets particularly animated most weekends when there's live Latin music. Also serves evening meals.

Bar da Cidade
Avenida do Infante. Daily 8pm–4am. A lively Brazilian music bar, with boppy sounds, a happy crowd, and scantily clad dancing girls.

Cais de Carvão
Jardins Panorámicos, Passeio Público Marítimo, ⓦ www.ccclube.com. Mon–Sat 11am–4am. This is the place to be seen in Funchal, attracting the city's rich and beautiful, with ultra-modern decor inside, and a choice of comfy sofas and armchairs on the outside terrace. Meals are served daily (except Monday evening) and it also hosts various club nights and special events; see the website for details.

Prince Albert
Rua Imperatriz Dona Amélia 86. Daily 11am–midnight. This English-style pub pulls in a loyal expat crowd (especially for its sports TV), along with young Madeirense

who pop in for a drink or two on the pre-clubbing circuit.

Pub No. 2

Rua da Favila 2. Daily 11am–2am. Charismatic, low-ceilinged bar comprising two wood-panelled rooms hung with agricultural implements. There's a small outside terrace, live soccer on the TV and a healthy mix of locals and tourists of all ages.

www.cyber Café

Avenida Infante 6. Mon–Tues 8am–1am, Wed–Sat 8am–4am. Lively cybercafé cum student bar, with a boisterous crowd thronging its small and intimate interior; karaoke nights Wednesday to Saturday from 11pm.

Clubs

Casino da Madeira

Rua Imperatriz Dona Amélia 55 ☎291 209 100, ⓦwww .casinodamadeira.com. Mon–Thurs & Sun 3pm–3am, Fri & Sat 4pm–4am. Free. Over-18s only. Funchal's circular concrete casino is part of a complex designed by Brazilian Oscar Niemeyer, the architect of Brasilia. From 8pm daily, there are slot machines, games of roulette and black

jack, along with cabaret, musical performances and special events in its various bars.

Jam

Avda Sá Carneiro 60 ☎291 234 800. Fri & Sat midnight–6am. An intimate disco attracting a retro crowd who like to get down to Gary Glitter, Abba and the like.

Marginal

Avenida Sá Carneiro ☎291 234 800. Fri & Sat midnight–6am. Facing the harbour, this is one of the smallest but most popular of the trio of clubs on this stretch. Alternative and house music rule the roost, with a high-energy, youthful clientele.

Vespas

Avenida Sá Carneiro 67 ☎291 234 800, ⓦwww.discotecavespas.com. Wed (Ladies' night) midnight–5.30am, Fri & Sat midnight–7am. Funchal's most popular nightclub, set in a gritty-looking former warehouse opposite the entrance to the harbour. The atmosphere is friendly, with a mainly young crowd dancing on the speakers. The minimum consumption policy of €125 a head isn't always adhered to, but be prepared.

Eastern Funchal and the Old Town

The area immediately east of the centre of Funchal is largely given over to bustling shopping streets, but it does contain a couple of notable sights: the engaging handicrafts museum IBTAM and the Museu de Franco, dedicated to the works of two local artists. Further east, the Mercado dos Lavradores, the central market, is one of Funchal's most characterful spots, and marks the beginning of the Zona Velha, or Old Town, with its bars, restaurants and atmospheric cobbled streets clustered round a seafront fort.

Praça do Carmo

Praça do Carmo is an attractive square full of outdoor café tables and surrounded by a warren of narrow pedestrianzed shopping streets. It takes its name from the pretty Igreja do Carmo, an eighteenth-century Baroque church, containing some fine azulejos and the tomb of the Conde de Carvalhal, the original owner of Quinta do Palheiro Ferreiro (see p.100).

Museu de Henrique e Francisco Franco

Rua de João de Deus. Mon–Fri 10am–12.30pm & 2–6pm. €2. Set in a 1940s building, the Museu de Henrique e Francisco Franco is dedicated to two of Madeira's most important modern artists, surprisingly little known internationally. The more famous of the two brothers, Franco – whose Monument to João Gonçalves Zarco graces Avenida Arriaga in the city centre – was born in Funchal in 1885. His career took off after he exhibited with Picasso in Boston in 1927, when his work attracted the attention of Portugal's dictator Salazar. Salazar commissioned Franco to create statues of great Portuguese heroes and, of course, himself. Many of these works are now in mainland Portugal, though a number are on display here, including the powerful *Torso de Mulher* (Body of a woman, 1922), heavily influenced by Rodin. What is most impressive about Franco's works is his wide range of styles, from classical to modern – see for example his tile designs and black–and–white pencil sketches;

▼ MUSEU DE HENRIQUE

▲ Airport/ Camacha

◁ Cable Car to Monte

P **Car Park**

Jardim
Botânico

Jardim
dos Loiros

CAMINHO DAS VEREDAS

NOVA

R. V. B

ESTRADA V. CACONGO

LOMBO DE BOA VISTA

MANUEL ALEXANDRE

RUA MAE DOS HOMENS

TRAVESSA

RUA DE SÃO FILIPE

Quinta da
Boa Vista

2

RUA NOVA DA ALEGRIA

R. NOVA
DA ROCHINHA

RUA DA ROCHINHA

CAMINHO DO MEIO

ESTRADA DA FIRA

RUA DA SILVA

Jardim
Orquídea

ESTRADA VISCONDE CACONGO

RUA MANUEL PESTANA JUNIOR

RUA RIBEIRA JOÃO GOMES

◁ Inset Box

▷ Main Map

RUA DAS
ROSAS

RUA DA ROCHINHA

R. NOVA DA ROCHINHA

CAMPO DA BARCA

ESTRADA C. DE CARVALHAS

ESTRADA CONSELHEIRO AIRES DE ORNELAS

RUA AROLPRESTE

RUA MIGUEL CARVALHO

LARGO
JAIME
MONIZ

RUA ORNELAS

RUA DA INFÂNCIA

RUA DO HOSPITAL VELHO

Police
Station
3

IBTAM

RUA MARY JANE WILSON

RUA DO VISCONDE DE ANADIA

RUA DO BRIGADEIRO OUDINOT

**Museu de Henrique
e Francisco Franco**

TRAVESSA DO REGO

a

RUA JOÃO DE DEUS

RUA ALFARES VEIGA PESTANA

RUA DAS HORTAS

**Anadia
Shopping
Centre &
Cinema**

RUA DO RIBEIRINHO

b

RUA DA FÁBRICA

RUA DO CARMO

RUA DAS HORTAS

3

RUA DO FRIGORÍFICO

LARGO DOS
LAVRADORES

RUA DO SEMINÁRIO

RUA DOUTOR FERNÃO DE ORNELAS

**Igreja do
Carmo**

1

PRAÇA DO
CARMO

LARGO
DO
PHELPS

TRAVESSA DA NOGUEIRA

RUA DA CONCEIÇÃO

R. F. PRETA

RUA DO BOM

R. F. REIS

RUA DA CONCEIÇÃO

R. P. J. DO ORNELAS

R. ELIAS GARCIA

RUA DA CONCEIÇÃO

TV. DO FORNO

AV. 5 DE

RUA BETTENCOURT

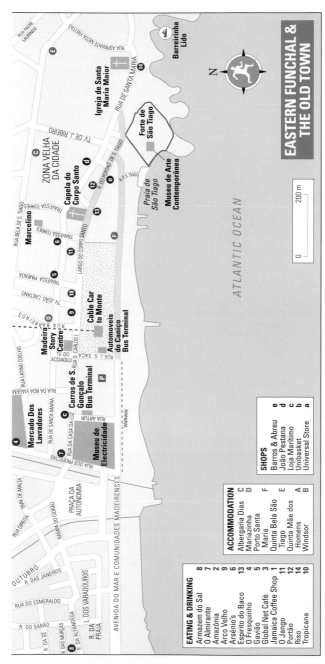

EASTERN FUNCHAL & THE OLD TOWN

PLACES

N

ATLANTIC OCEAN

0 — 200 m

EATING & DRINKING

Armazem do Sal	8
O Almirante	7
Amazónia	2
Arco Velho	9
Arsénio's	6
Espirito do Baco	13
O Fresquinho	4
Gavião	5
Global Net Café	3
Jamaica Coffee Shop	1
O Jango	11
Portão	12
Riso	14
Tropicana	10

ACCOMMODATION

Albergaria Dias	C
Mariazinha	D
Porto Santa Maria	F
Quinta Bela São Tiago	E
Quinta Mãe dos Homens	A
Windsor	B

SHOPS

Barros & Abreu	e
João Pestana	d
Loja Marítimo	c
Unibasket	b
Universal Store	a

Buses from Funchal

Details of buses from Funchal are given in the relevant town accounts, including average journey times from the capital. Many of Funchal's bus companies use the Zona Velha as their departure point – a full list of all Funchal's bus terminals is given on p.192.

look out, too, for the evocative, minimalist *Cena do Café* (Scene in a café, 1923). The museum also contains works by Franco's brother, Henriques, a highly respected painter in his own right, known for his portrayal of scenes from Madeiran everyday life.

IBTAM

Rua do Visconde de Anadia 44. Mon–Fri 10am–12.30pm & 2.30–5.30pm. €2. The Instituto de Bordados Tapeçaria e Artesanato de Madeira (Institute of Embroidery, Tapestry and Craftsmanship of Madeira), or IBTAM, was set up in 1978 to monitor standards of Madeira's longstanding handicrafts industry and provide training. The tradition of embroidery, in particular, goes back a long way, a continuation of a skill practised in Portuguese

convents since the Middle Ages. The upper floor is now a handicrafts museum and the varied exhibits and photographs give some insight into the importance of crafts to the island's art and culture. Perhaps the most interesting exhibit – if only for its size – is an enormous tapestry entitled *Allegory of Madeira*, hung in the main hallway, halfway up the stairs. It took over three years to complete, from 1958 to 1961. Other highlights include an Irish linen cloth embroidered by Madeirans for Queen Elizabeth II's visit to Lisbon in 1957 and a bedchamber as it would have looked in the nineteenth century.

Mercado dos Lavradores

Main entrance on Largo dos Lavradores. Mon–Thurs 7am–4pm, Fri 7am–8pm, Sat 7am–2pm. Funchal's

▼ MERCADO DOS LAVRADORES

vibrant main market, the Mercado dos Lavradores, sells a colourful array of fish, exotic fruits and local crafts. Housed in a yellow building faced with azulejos, it was designed in the 1930s by Edmundo Tavares, one of Portugal's best-known twentieth-century architects. Much of its appeal lies in the theatrical air lent by the tiers of arcades, thronged with shoppers looking down on the activity in the central courtyard below. The lower tier contains counter after counter of scabbard fish, vast octopi, tuna steaks the size of frisbees and other weird-looking Atlantic fish. The main ground-floor area is a medley of stalls selling vegetables, exotic fruit and wickerwork. The upper floor has more fruit and vegetables, along with dried chillies, clothes and caged birds.

Museu de Electricidade

Rua da Casa da Luz 2. Tues–Sat 10am–12.30pm & 2–6pm. €2. Set in the high-ceilinged, former Central Power Station of Funchal, the Museu de Electricidade is a surprisingly engaging museum charting the history of electricity and lighting in Madeira and illustrated with dials, generators, photos, illustrations and real street lamps. You learn that the British ran the first electricity supply in 1897 (it was not until the end of the World War II that power was literally in the hands of the local council) and how during the war, electricity shortages made it necessary to develop water-powered generators, leading to hydro-electric power in the 1950s, still one of the primary sources of energy on the island today.

Madeira Story Centre

Rua Dom Carlos I 27–29 ⓦ www .storycentre.com. Daily 10am–6pm. €10, children under 14 €5. Set in a former cinema, the Madeira Story Centre neatly encapsulates the island's history through a series of models, pictures and multimedia displays. Don't expect anything flash or high-tech, but the life-size model pirates, great black-and-white TV footage of the island and details of the early flying boats just about warrant the steep entry fees. There's also a roof terrace with activities for kids and a well-stocked shop.

The cable car to Monte

Daily: 9.30am–5.45pm. €10 single, €14.50 return. The high-tech cable car to Monte starts in the grassy mini-park in front of the old town. The ten-minute ride is exhilarating, the glass bubbles of the cable car swaying between huge green metal pillars erected high over Funchal's buildings.

The Old Town

The Old Town, or Zona Velha, is an atmospheric area of cobbled streets, dotted with flowering mimosa trees and lined with former fishermen's houses, some dating back to the first colonization of Funchal in the fifteenth century. Though it's filled with restaurants firmly geared to tourists, in the evenings, locals chat on the doosteps and children play in the street.

The focal point of the area is Largo do Corpo Santo, on one side of which sits the small sixteenth-century Capela do Corpo Santo, believed to be one of the oldest chapels on the island and dedicated to São Pedro, the patron saint of fishermen.

Forte de São Tiago and the Museu de Arte Contemporânea

Mon–Sat 10am–12.30pm & 2–5.30pm. €2.50. Set on a little rocky outcrop overlooking the sea is the Forte de São Tiago, with its distinctive ochre walls. Built in 1614 to defend the city from pirate attack, the structure later became what must have been a cramped home to 3500 British troops, stationed in Funchal during the Napoleonic wars. Britain was keen to protect its commercial interests in Madeira from the French, who briefly occupied mainland Portugal before the British pushed them back. In 1803, the fort was again occupied when it became a temporary shelter to the thousands of locals made homeless by the devastating floods which hit the capital. It now houses a couple of small and rather uninspiring museums, though it's worth the admission price just to wander round its rambling ramparts.

Overlooking the courtyard is the Military Room, containing a tiny, rather dull collection of military maps, illustrations and weapons. You're better off following the arrows to the former military governor's house, which since 1992 has been occupied by the **Museu de Arte Contemporânea**, a rather hit-and-miss collection of contemporary Portuguese art from 1960 to the present. Highlights include some interesting photographic works by Helena Almeida (1971) on the top floor, and some attractive work by Pedro Cabrita Ries, notably *Naturália Parte 6* (1996), along with Rui Sanches' cracked tile effects in pale blue and white on the floor below. The bottom floor displays some colourful works by Eduardo de Freitas, one of the few Madeiran artists on show.

Praia de São Tiago

Just by the entrance to the fort, Rua Portão São Tiago leads to the Praia de São Tiago, a stony little beach. Locals swim off it in summer and use the concrete terrace behind for sunbathing. There's also a tiny seasonal kiosk café serving cold beers.

▼ FORTE DE SÃO TIAGO

The Barreirinha Lido

Daily 9am–6pm. €1.60, extra charges for use of chairs and sun umbrellas. Bus #40 from Avenida do Mar. Set under the cliffs is the modest Barreirinha Lido, comprising a gym, changing rooms and a shallow seawater pool, which is great for kids. Swimming is better in summer, when you can swim off a small stony beach out to temporary diving platforms moored out to sea.

Igreja de Santa Maria Maior

Rua de Santa Maria. The Baroque seventeenth-century Igreja de Santa Maria Maior is one of the most attractive churches in the city. Also known as Igreja de São Tiago or Socorro, the church was built on the site of an earlier chapel constructed to commemorate the plague of 1538. There is still a procession every May 1 in honour of the plague victims.

Jardim Botânico

Caminho do Meio. Daily 9am–5.30pm. €3. Buses #29 and #30 from Largo dos Lavradores/Rua da Infância or bus #31 from opposite the marina. Also cable car from Monte; see below. The city's Jardim Botânico (Botanical Garden) comprises an evocative series of lawns, woods and grottoes, offering stupendous views over the city and also containing its own natural history museum, parrot park and pricey café. The grounds were once part of a private estate, the Quinta do Bom Successo, owned by the Reid family (see p.72), who laid out the gardens as a private park. The gardens contain some two thousand exotic plant species from five continents, including papyrus grass, anthurium and bird-of-paradise – although most plants are either indigenous or from the Azores,

▲ JARDIM BOTÂNICO

Cape Verde or the Canaries. Don't miss the extraordinary collection of cacti and succulents, ranging from tiny, flowering cacti to enormous spiky specimens, their spines draped in cobwebs.

Close to the park entrance is the **Museu de História Natural** (daily 9am–5.30pm), a rather quaint collection of pickled fish, dusty stuffed birds, mammals and fossils, collected from round the island. The highlight is a giant, ten-million-year-old fossilized tree heather, found in an underground cavern that was discovered during tunnelling for one of Madeira's new roads. At the foot of the gardens you'll hear the squawks from the **Jardim dos Loiros** (Parrot Garden), a colourful array of tropical birds, including macaws, green and crimson parakeets and salmon-crested cockatoos.

Jardim Botânico cable car

Caminho do Meio. Daily 9.30am–6pm. €7.75 single, €12.25 return. Buses #29 and #30 from Largo dos Lavradores/ Rua da Infância. Reached from the northernmost point of the Botanical Gardens is another vertiginous cable car, part of a new complex of shops with its own café. The cable car passes high over the wooded João Gomes river valley to just below Monte in around ten minutes. To get to or from the cable car without paying to enter the Botanical Gardens, head along the steep Caminho do Meio, five to ten minutes' walk above the main Botanical Gardens entrance. The cable car is reached via a lift from the car park.

Jardim Orquídea

Rua Pita da Silva 37. ⓦ www .madeiraorchids.com. Daily 9.30am–6pm. €5. Buses #29 and #30 from Largo dos Lavradores/Rua da Infância or #31 from opposite the marina. The Jardim Orquídea (Orchid Garden) consists of small areas of covered and semi-covered gardens sheltering a riot of weirdly shaped and coloured orchids, intermingled with other plants and the odd exotic bird. The main flowering season is from November to April, though some of the four

thousand varieties can usually be seen in bloom at other times. True orchid lovers can find out about the technicalities of the flowers' cultivation, explained here in great detail. If you want to buy a plant (packaged in easily transportable glass jars), those suitable for growing in colder climates are well labelled. There's also a small café with sweeping city views.

Quinta da Boa Vista

Rua Lombo da Boa Vista 25. Mon–Sat 9am–6pm. €3.50. Bus #32 from Avenida do Mar to the end of the line, then a five-minute walk downhill. The attractive eighteenth-century Quinta Boa Vista is owned by the former Honorary British Consul to Madeira and contains one of Madeira's most important collections of orchids, featuring many rare species. Covered areas under green gauze shelter row upon row of potted orchids in a spectacular range of shapes and colours. It's best to come early, as it can get crowded. Just below the orchid houses there is a lovely garden set out with tables and chairs, where tea and cake are sometimes served.

▼ QUINTA DA BOA VISTA

Hotels

Albergaria Dias

Rua Bela São Tiago 44b ☏ 291 206 680, ⓦ www.albergariadias.com. Small and friendly four-star hotel in a tranquil position (though off a busy road) with 35 plush rooms, most with sea views (€30 extra). In summer, breakfast is served in the small garden with its own pool. There's also a gym and sauna, though you'll pay extra to use them. €100.

Residencial da Mariazinha

Rua de Santa Maria 155 ☏ 291 220 239, ⓦ www.residencialmariazinha.com. In the heart of the Zona Velha, this beautifully renovated town house has good-sized rooms decked out in contemporary style. There's also a large breakfast room, bar and patio. €70.

Hotel Porto Santa Maria

Avenida do Mar 50 ☏ 291 206 700, ⓦ www.portobay.com. Superbly positioned, if somewhat bland, four-star on the edge of the Old Town, facing the sea. Rooms are spacious – all have kitchenettes and the best ones face the waves. There are also indoor and outdoor pools, a restaurant, bar, sauna and gym, and breakfast can be taken on the terrace. €200.

Quinta Bela São Tiago

Rua Bela São Tiago 70 ☏ 291 204 500, ⓦ www.hotel-qta-bela-s-tiago .com. Just a stone's throw from the Zona Velha, this stunning quinta of 1894 has been tastefully extended with two modern wings. Most rooms have balconies facing the spires of the Old Town and the sea, and there's also a pool, terrace and small garden, along with a gym, sauna, jacuzzi, restaurant and bar – a great place to watch the sun set. €260.

Quinta Mãe dos Homens

Rua Mãe dos Homens 39 ☏ 291 204 410, ⓦ www.qmdh.com. Small and highly recommended complex of spotless, roomy self-catering studios and apartments set behind an old quinta amidst a mini banana plantation in the attractive residential suburb of Rochinha. There's a pool, honesty bar and weekly barbecue evenings. The only drawback is the steep fifteen-minute climb uphill from the centre, though its lofty position commands great vistas and it's also conveniently close to the Botanical Gardens. Breakfast not included. €92.

Hotel Windsor

Rua das Hortas 4C ☏ 291 233 081, ⓦ www.hotelwindsorgroup.pt. This neo-Art Deco block has unevenly shaped rooms, none of which is particularly big, but the location is very central, the atmosphere is friendly, and there's a small café and restaurant downstairs, plus a rooftop pool. €70.

Shops

Barros & Abreu Irmãos Peles e Botas

Rua do Portão de São Tiago 22–23. Mon–Fri 9am–1pm & 3–7pm, Sat 9am–1pm. A traditional family workshop where typical Madeiran *cordovo* (goatskin boots) are made to measure on the premises at very reasonable rates.

João Pestana

Rua de Santa Maria 233–235. Mon–Fri 10am–5.30pm. Titchy

workshop producing beautifully crafted boater hats, bags and other crafts, mostly aimed at tourists.

Loja Marítimo

Rua Dom Carlos 13. Mon–Fri 10am–2pm & 3–6pm, Sat 9am–noon. The merchandising outlet for the city's most successful soccer team, selling official replica kits and tickets for matches. The adjacent museum displays Marítimo's trophies, pennants and photographs, with pride of place given to the 1925–26 Portuguese Championship trophy.

Unibasket

Rua do Carmo 44. Mon–Fri 10am–1pm & 2–7pm, Sat 10am–1pm. A large store with a big yard out the back stashed with quality household goods from Madeira and the east, including ceramics, statues, furniture and a large range of wicker chairs and baskets.

Universal Store

Rua de João de Deus 14a. Mon–Sat 9.30am–7.30pm, Sun 9.30am–1.30pm. Handicrafts emporium set in a former Protestant church. Prices aren't particularly cheap but it offers a wide range of goods including embroidery, leather belts, pottery, azulejos, clothes and children's toys, while the basement is stuffed with an enormous selection of wines.

Cafés

Arco Velho

Rua Dom Carlos I 42. Daily 8am– midnight. Lively café, especially busy on a Sunday morning when locals gather here to read the Sunday papers over pastries, coffee and drinks. There's an outdoor terrace from where you can watch the capsules pass overhead on the Funchal– Monte cable car.

O Fresquinho

Mercado dos Lavradores. Mon–Fri 8am–8pm, Sat 8am–2pm. The most atmospheric of the market's café-bars, set in the front of the upper floor with a stand-up bar area and a few tables set to the

▼ RUA DE SANTA MARIA

side surrounded by plants and hemmed in by stalls selling fruit and plucked chickens. Sells sandwiches, snacks, beers and coffee.

Global Net Café

Rua Hospital Velho 25A. Mon–Fri 10am–8pm, Sat 10am–2pm. Fashionable little cybercafé opposite the market, with ten terminals (€2.50 an hour) and fine coffee.

Jamaica Coffee Shop

Praça do Carmo. Mon–Sat 8am–midnight. Attractive café under the arches of the Praça do Carmon, with outdoor tables spilling onto the square and a good range of coffee, tea and cold drinks.

▲ THE DAY'S CATCH IN THE OLD TOWN

Restaurants

O Almirante

Largo do Poço 1–3 ☏ 291 224 252. Daily 8am–midnight. The beautiful first-floor dining room features wood beams, chandeliers and high-backed chairs – a lovely spot to enjoy *bacalhau* and other fish, lobster, squid, kebabs and dishes such as *Fidago ao Madeira* (Madeiran liver). There's also a good *pastelaria* section downstairs. Mains from €14.

Armazem do Sal

Rua da Alfandega 135 ☏ 291 241 285. Mon–Fri noon–midnight, Sat 7pm–midnight. Set in a stone-clad former salt warehouse, this is one of central Funchal's more fashionable restaurants, with sleek service and a small patio area. The menu features local ingredients with an international twist, such as tuna with risotto. Around €20 for a full meal.

Arsénio's

Rua da Santa Maria 169 ☏ 291 224 007. Daily 7pm–midnight. Highly rated for its fish and meat dishes, with an outdoor grill wafting mouthwatering smells to the tables under the covered terrace. Most people head here for the nightly fado sessions in the azulejos-lined interior, which bumps up the prices, but at least the fado is more authentic than the cheesy warm-up musicians on electric keyboards. It's one of the Old Town's most popular dining spots, so get there early or book ahead.

Gavião

Rua de Santa Maria 131 ☏ 291 229 238. Daily noon–11pm. Very popular but small restaurant – go early or book ahead to guarantee a table. The menu features a long list of meat dishes and salads, but most people cram in for some of the best fresh fish in Funchal, served by the friendly owner. The mixed fish grill is superb. Around €15–20 for a full meal.

O Jango
Rua de Santa Maria 166 ⓣ291 221 280. Daily 11am–11pm. Small split-level restaurant shoe-horned into a former fisherman's house with simple, excellent-value grilled fish dishes – though other dishes tend to be smothered in rich sauces and served with over-boiled vegetables. Clam *cataplana*, *gambas a Indiana* (Indian-style prawns) and the house wine are also good. Mains from €12.

Portão
Rua do Portão de São Tiago ⓣ291 221 125. Tues–Sun noon–midnight. This restaurant has outdoor tables and an attractive interior, decorated with mock wood beams and azulejos. Service is friendly and unpretentious and the fish, meat and the *bacalhau* dishes are good value, at around €10.

Riso
Rua de Santa Maria 274 ⓣ291 280 360. Daily 12.30am–2.30pm & 7–10.30pm, café 10am–6pm. Swish and minimalist, with a fantastic terrace overlooking the Barreirinho Lido, *Riso* specializes in dishes made using rice – which features even the desserts and starters. The menu includes fantastic risottos (including those with prawns and mussels, and scabbard fish with lime and banana), plus

"world" rice dishes such as paella, curries and salmon with Thai rice, though don't expect much change from €30 a head.

Marisqueira Tropicana
Rua Dom Carlos I 43 ⓣ291 225 705. Daily 10am–1pm. More reasonably priced than many of the restaurants on this stretch of Rua Dom Carlos, with good-value tuna, fish and Portuguese dishes. There's also a pleasant street-facing terrace.

Bars

Amazónia
Rua de São Felipe 19 ⓣ291 228 164. Daily 4pm–2am. Very popular with a young crowd, this friendly bar has tropical decor and thumping music. The volume is lower in the lovely garden, a great spot to nurse a drink or two.

Espirito do Baco
Largo do Corpo Santo 28–30 ⓣ291 282 159. Mon–Sat noon–midnight, Sun 6pm–midnight. This tiny split-level wine bar serves a range of wines and Madeiras accompanied by tasty tapas-like snacks and cheese boards, with low stools inside or out. Also serves tea and cakes.

Live music

Marcelino
Travessa das Torres 22a ⓣ291 220 216. Daily 9pm–2am. Set in a low-ceilinged traditional building, this fado house is the best place in town to sample the traditional Portuguese version of the blues, nightly at 10pm. Also a nice spot to down a beer or two.

Monte and northeast of Funchal

One of the easiest and most rewarding half-day trips from Funchal is to Monte, a hilltop town overlooking the capital and site of some spectacular gardens. Getting to and from Monte can be half the fun: up on a cable car and down on an exhilarating dry toboggan run. To the east lies Quinta do Palheiro Ferreiro – more popularly known as Blandy's – a must for garden lovers, with a riot of tropical plants set in extensive grounds. All these places are accessible by public transport, but are also connected by paths and the Levada dos Tornos, which makes a gentle introduction to Madeira's spectacular walks.

Monte

Funchal city buses #20, #21 and #60 from Praça da Autonomia, and #48 from the Hotel Zone; also by cable car from the Zona Velha (see p.85) or the Jardim Botânico (see p.87). The attractive hilltop town of Monte perches 550m above sea level, a six-kilometre climb northeast of Funchal. Its wooded slopes, cool air and dramatic views established it in the mid-nineteenth century as a healthy retreat for the island's wealthy residents and as a popular base for transatlantic passengers stopping off in Madeira. Numerous quintas were built in and around the town to put visitors up before the first hotel appeared in Funchal at the end of the nineteenth century. After World War II, Monte's fortunes fell as Funchal took over as the main centre for tourism, though it has remained one of the most popular excursions from the capital. Most visitors arrive by one of two cable cars (see p.85 & p.87), both of which terminate off Caminho das Barbosas, near the entrance to the Jardins Tropicais do Monte Palace (see p.96); to reach the main square, Largo da Fonte, turn left and continue down Caminho das Barbosas for around 200m.

▼ CABLE CAR TO MONTE

Largo da Fonte

Most buses from Funchal stop by Largo da Fonte, centred on a little bandstand, overlooking the verdant Parque do Monte public gardens, which spread down the gully below. The park is bordered to the east by parts of the old viaduct of a defunct rack-and-pinion railway, whose arches are covered in vegetation. There a plans to re-create the final stretch of the railway which connected Funchal via Monte to Terreiro da Luta. The original steam-powered engines, built in 1893, proved alarmingly prone to exploding – four people were killed in one incident in 1919 – and it was discontinued in 1939. To the east of the square is the Fonte da Virgem, a little fountain with a shrine to Nossa Senhora do Monte.

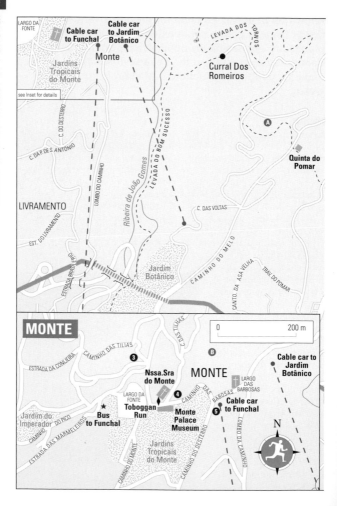

Quinta Jardins do Imperador

Caminho do Pico. Mon–Sat 9.30am–
5.30pm. €6. Originally laid out in
1826 as the summer residence
of English merchant James
Gordon, the quinta is best
known for being the final home
of Emperor Karl I of Austria
and King of Hungary, the last
Habsburg monarch. Karl was
married to Princess Zita, the
granddaughter of Dom Miguel I
of Portugal. In 1922 the
emperor was banished from his
homeland and came to Madeira
with Zita in the hope that the
warm climate would improve
his health. He lived here for a
year before dying of pneumonia,
aged 35. His body lies in Nossa
Senhora do Monte (see p.96).
His former home is undergoing
restoration, but you can wander
round the extensive grounds,

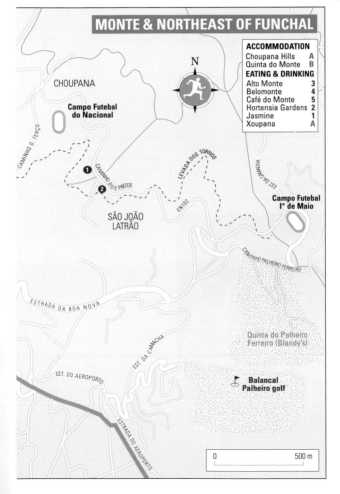

MONTE & NORTHEAST OF FUNCHAL

N

ACCOMMODATION
Choupana Hills   A
Quinta do Monte   B
EATING & DRINKING
Alto Monte   3
Belomonte   4
Café do Monte   5
Hortensia Gardens   2
Jasmine   1
Xoupana   A

CHOUPANA

Campo Futebal
do Nacional

CAMINHO D. TERÇO

CAMINHO DOS PRETOS

LEVADA DOS TORNOS

EN 102

EST. DA CANÇADA

Campo Futebal
I° de Maio

SÃO JOÃO
LATRÃO

CAMINHO PALHEIRO FERREIRO

ESTRADA DA BOA NOVA

Quinta do Palheiro
Ferreiro (Blandy's)

EST. DA CAMACHA

EST. DO AEROPORTO

Balancal
Palheiro golf

ESTRADA DO AEROPORTO

0   500 m

refreshingly informal and studded with trees and vibrant agapanthus. There's also a small café set in a nineteenth-century folly turret by a small lake.

Nossa Senhora do Monte

The twin-towered Nossa Senhora do Monte (Our Lady of the Mountain) is the island's most important church and stands on the site of one of Madeira's first chapels, built in 1470 by Adam Gonçalves Ferreira, one of a pair of twins (his sister was called Eve) who, appropriately enough, were the first children born on the island. The original chapel was levelled in the 1748 earthquake and was replaced in 1818 by the current Baroque structure, an attractive building with low-hanging chandeliers and a painted ceiling.

The altar displays a particularly revered statue of the Virgin, found by a shepherdess in nearby Terreira da Luta (see p.98) in

▼ NOSSA SENHORA DO MONTE

the fifteenth century; azulejos panels on the front of the church depict the moment of discovery. During the Feast of Assumption on August 14–15, pilgrims climb the church's 74 rough basalt steps on their knees to pay homage to the Virgin – a feat which looks as painful as it sounds – before the statue is taken out and processed. Far less solemn is the *romaria* in the evening, a festival with music and fireworks.

The church is also the final resting place of Emperor Karl I of Austria and King of Hungary, who lived for a time in the Quinta do Imperador (see p.95). Deposed in 1918 at the end of World War I after just two years in power, in 2004, he was sanctified by the Pope for his efforts to end the war. His tomb is on the left of the altar in a rather spartan side room.

Jardins Tropicais do Monte Palace

Caminho do Monte 174 Ⓦ www .montepalace.com. Daily 9.30am–6pm. €10. If you visit just one garden on Madeira, you should make it the Jardins Tropicais do Monte Palace, as much a museum as a garden, filled with fountains, statues and works of art, as well as around a hundred thousand species of plants. The gardens spill down seventeen acres of verdant ravine towards the eighteenth-century building that is home to the park's owner, José Rodrigues Berardo, a local tobacco magnate and one of Portugal's leading arts benefactors. As well as setting up the park's imaginative range of exhibits, he has introduced to the gardens rare cycads – prehistoric tree ferns (cicas) from South Africa (there are now more examples of this species here than anywhere

▲ JARDINS TROPICAIS DO MONTE PALACE

else in the world) – azaleas and heathers from northern Europe and indigenous plants from Madeira.

The entrance fee includes access to the **Monte Palace Museum** (daily 10.30am–3.30pm), by the entrance, displaying petrified wood, over a thousand African stone carvings and a similar number of semi-precious stones from around the world. From the entrance, paths descend past koi fish ponds down a series of steps into the ravine. One path is lined with decorative modern azulejos panels, each showing key moments in Portugal's history – the most dramatic is the one depicting the Great Earthquake in Lisbon in 1755, which is followed by a series showing the rebuilding of the capital. Just beyond here, a formal Japanese-style garden shelters 166 colourful glazed panels tracing the 450-year trading alliance between Portugal and Japan.

Further down the slope spectacular plants form the backdrop to a lake and the world's largest ceramic vase, which stands 5.345m high and weighs 555 kilos. Southeast of the lake, a path leads down to the park café.

The toboggan run

Carreiros do Monte. Mon–Sat 9am–6pm, Sun 9am–1pm. €20 for

Manueline architecture

Manueline architecture is a uniquely Portuguese style of architecture which emerged during the reign of Manuel I (1495–1521) and developed from the Gothic. The early sixteenth century was the age of Portugal's maritime discoveries and these provided the inspiration for Manueline motifs, drawn from ships' masts, ropes, anchors and the exotic animal and plant life encountered abroad, and which frequently adorned windows, doors and columns. Many of Madeira's earliest buildings incorporated elements of Manueline architecture; some of the best examples are to be found in Funchal's Quinta das Cruzes (see p.61) and the Jardins Tropicais do Monte Palace in Monte (see opposite).

▲ PREPARING THE TOBOGGAN RUN

one person, €25 for two, €38 for three. For most people, the toboggan run is the most memorable experience to be had in Monte. You'll see the dapper-looking drivers lined up on the street beneath the church in pristine white shirts, with straw boaters and goatskin boots. The toboggans are basically giant wicker baskets, known as *carros de cesto* (basket cars), attached to wooden runners. Until the mid-nineteenth century, similar baskets were pulled up and down the slopes by horses and bullocks, but in 1850 they were adapted so that two drivers could control their descent to transport produce to the town's market, as well as carrying local landowners. They quickly became popular with visiting tourists – Ernest Hemingway, who had his fair share of adventures, described the ride as one of the most exhilarating experiences in his life.

The drivers get you going with the aid of ropes, hopping onto the back as you pick up speed. It can be pretty scary as you plummet downhill, though in fact you are not going as fast as it feels, and the baskets are easily stopped: the drivers' goatskin boots have special rubber-treaded soles that act as brakes. The baskets are manoeuvred over manhole covers and past potholes in the road; the most alarming bit is when the sleds occasionally start to veer off at an angle, a sign that the runners need extra oil.

Rides last about ten minutes and end up a couple of kilometres downhill in the suburb of Livramento, where there are a couple of cafés, a bus stop and usually a taxi waiting to take people back into Funchal.

Terreiro da Luta

From Monte take São Gonçalo bus #103 (2 daily), bus #138 (Mon–Sat 1 daily), or #56 (Mon–Fri 2 daily, Sun 1 daily). The impressive hillside monument of Terreiro da Luta marks the spot where a local shepherdess found the revered statue of the Virgin, now in Nossa Senhora do Monte (see p.96). Composed of an elaborate stone column supporting a statue of the Virgin, the monument was built in 1927 as a memorial to the end of World War I. At the height of the war in 1916, Madeira came under attack from German submarines, during which a French ship was hit, killing several people. The Madeirans prayed at the altar of the church in Monte and vowed to build the statue if the war was stopped. This they duly did and today, at the foot of

A walk from Monte to the Jardim Botânico

This relatively gentle walk, taking 90–120 minutes, follows footpaths, a *levada* and steep roads, offering superb views over Funchal en route. It covers parts of the Levada dos Tornos walk from Quinta do Palheiro Ferreiro detailed in the opposite direction on p.101.

From Monte, head east past the entrance to the Funchal cable car and continue straight on past the second cable car to the Jardim Botânico. You're now on the track signed Curral dos Romeiros. A cobbled path takes you down, round and up a wooded steep valley, and in thirty minutes you'll arrive in the little village of Curral dos Romeiros. Head through the village on the main track, and you'll see steps on the left signed Levada dos Tornos/Camacha. Take these and follow the *levada* path, which winds through eucalyptus woods; after around thirty minutes you'll pass the log cabins of the *Choupana Hills* resort. Continue along the *levada* and in another ten minutes you'll reach a road. Turn right and head steeply downhill. The main road veers left after 150m or so, but carry on down a very steep, semi-stepped cobbled track – you'll now see Funchal below you. After five minutes you'll reach a junction with two restaurants on your right. If you have strong knees, you can continue straight on down the steep Caminho do Meio, which will bring you out in front of the Jardim Botânico (see p.87) after another five to ten minutes. Alternatively, turn right at the junction along the busier Caminho das Voltas, which winds more gently downhill – bus #29 (every 30min) passes along this stretch on its way into Funchal – and after twenty minutes you'll come out by the Jardim Botânico's entrance.

the statue, you can still see the anchor chains from the French ship that was destroyed in the bombardment.

By the road junction near the statue is the terminus of the former Funchal–Monte railway line (there are plans to re open the final section from Monte). The old station building, dating from 1912, is currently a restaurant school.

By bus, ask for Terreiro da Luta and you'll be dropped 200m or so from the statue; alternatively, a taxi from Monte costs around €6 one-way. The walk back down to Monte is well worth doing. Take the steep cobbled track next to the old station building, heading downhill past stations of the cross, with a distant

Funchal as a backdrop. Yellow and red markers direct you along the Caminha das Laginhas – past traditional village houses

▲ TERREIRO DA LUTA MONUMENT

– and onto the Caminho do Monte in Monte, around twenty minutes' walk.

Quinta do Palheiro Ferreiro (Blandy's)

Mon–Fri 9am–4.30pm. €9. Horários do Funchal city bus #36A (5 daily) or #37 (Mon–Fri 1 daily) from Praça da Autonomia. Better known as Blandy's, the estate of Quinta do Palheiro Ferreiro is a must if you like formal gardens. The thirty-acre estate was founded by the Portuguese Count of Carvalhal in the early nineteenth century, when a quinta and the Baroque chapel were built in the middle of formal gardens and the grounds stocked with deer. Later, during the Miguelite uprising, the Count was forced to flee Madeira for England, and when he returned to the island, he introduced some of the gardening techniques he had encountered there – at 550m in altitude, the cool climate is similar to Britain's, allowing trees such as oaks, beech and chestnuts to thrive. He also introduced ornamental ponds and planted camellia trees as wind breaks – these produce vivid red flowers from December to around April and are now one of the garden's highlights.

In 1884 the estate was bought out by the powerful Blandy family, who had settled in Madeira after the Napoleonic wars and stayed on to set

▼ CHURCH OF BARBOSAS, MONTE

A walk from Quinta do Palheiro Ferreiro to Monte

From Quinta do Palheiro Ferreiro you can easily join the central section of the Levada dos Tornos, Madeira's newest *levada*, and follow it to Monte – about a two-hour walk, if you don't stop at either of the two tea houses en route. Though not one of Madeira's prettiest *levadas*, it is the most accessible from Funchal and a good taster for other *levada* walks.

To reach the *levada*, turn right out of the Quinta do Palheiro Ferreiro and head uphill until you come to a junction (by two small cafés), where you turn left. Follow the road for 100m, after which the *levada* is clearly signposted on the left. At first, the *levada* passes close by the busy EN102 road above an unattractive block of council houses, but it soon plunges into shady, sweet-smelling eucalyptus woods, all the time running roughly parallel to the road, and crossing it at one stage.

After twenty minutes you pass the *Jasmine Tea House* (see p.102); there's another café, *Hortensia Gardens Tea House* (see p.102), ten minutes' further on.

The *levada* then follows the contours of the valley away from the road beneath more towering eucalyptus trees. Eventually you cross a steep road and pass a small weir just before a manor house, Quinta do Pomar. The path skirts the back of the quinta and rejoins the *levada*. Just past here you cross a road and within ten minutes you pass through the *Choupana Hills* resort. The *levada* continues through eucalyptus woods for another thirty minutes, when steps down to your left take you to the little village of Curral dos Romeiros. Head straight on through the village on the main track, where a wooden sign points you onto a cobbled track to Monte. The track winds down, round and up a steep, wooded valley before arriving by the cable car from the Jardim Botânico, a couple of minutes' walk from the top of the Funchal cable car in Monte.

up Blandy's Madeira Wine Company in Funchal. The Blandys added plants from round the world, and continue to run the estate today.

Buses drop you at the entrance to the gardens, from where a cobbled track leads down to the left past the back of the old quinta building to a coach and taxi rank. Just in front of the quinta you'll see the original chapel, with stained-glass windows in the turret casting coloured light over the bright walls. Beyond here, the public areas consist of a series of formal flowerbeds, topiary, ponds and lush lawns, which combine the formal English style with a tropical exuberance, epitomized by the mingling of blackbird song with the hum of cicadas.

Less formal is the untended, overgrown ravine to the west of the gardens, known as the Inferno: a path leads down into a valley full of giant ferns and trailing morning glory vines before snaking back up to the entrance.

Balancal Palheiro Golf

Rua do Balancal 29, São Gonçalo ☏ 291 790 125, ⓦ www.palheirogolf .com. Horários do Funchal city bus #33 from Praça da Autonomia. Opened in 1994, the eighteen-hole Balancal Palheiro Golf was designed by Cabel Robinson and is one of the most spectacularly sited in Europe, known for its tight fairways and fast greens. It lies adjacent to the grounds of the exclusive hotel belonging to the estate, the *Casa Velha do Palheiro*. If you don't mind paying through the nose, you can take tea or drinks in the hotel bar or on the lawns in front.

Hotels

Choupana Hills

Travessa do Largo da Choupana, Choupana ☏291 206 020, ⓦwww .choupanahills.com. Deluxe spa hotel set in rural isolation with a fantastic view over Funchal. Rooms are in Eastern-influenced wooden bungalows with balconies while, inside, the low furniture contributes to a Zen-like calm. The pagoda-like main building contains a designer bar (which hosts a jazz festival in September), restaurant (see p.103) top-of-the-range spa facilities plus indoor and outdoor pools. The latter overlooks the Levada dos Tornos, which passes right through the grounds. €300 (inland views) up to €315 for sea views.

Quinta do Monte

Caminho do Monte 192, Monte ☏291 780 100, ⓦwww.charminghotels madeira.com. Most of the rooms at this lovely hotel above the Jardins Tropicais do Monte are in a modern extension of an old quinta, which retains its sumptuous grounds. Rooms are large and in contemporary style with balconies, cable TV and air conditioning – the best ones face the distant Atlantic. The original quinta now houses a bar and lounge, while other communal facilities include a pool, gym and Turkish bath. €160.

Cafés

Hortensia Gardens Tea House

Caminho dos Pretos 89, São João Latrão. Daily 9am–6pm. Signposted off the Levada dos Tornos and by the stop for bus #47 to Funchal, this place boasts lovely gardens, a couple of terraces and an attractive interior with superb vistas. It also offers a wide range of Portuguese food along with home-baked bread, tea and scones.

Jasmine Tea House

Caminho dos Pretos 40, São João Latrão. May–Sept 10am–6pm,

▼ HORTENSIA TEA HOUSE

Oct–April 10am–5pm.
A well-known
English-run tea
house which cashes
in on its position
on the *levada* walk.
Reached by a series
of steep steps, it
seems to have been
beamed in from
some coastal town
in southern England,
complete with corny
wall signs, framed
cartoons and a
patio garden with ornamental
fountain. Dishes include tea and
scones, some good broth-like
soups and an impressive range of
fruit and herbal teas.

▲ TEA BREAK ON THE LEVADA WALK

Café do Parque
Largo Da Fonte, Monte. Daily
9am–6pm. A café-cum-souvenir
shop right on the main square,
serving light meals (from around
€7) and hot and cold drinks,
including a fine range of milk
shakes. There's a roof terrace,
though the best tables are those
outside on the square itself.

Restaurants

Alto Monte
Travessa das Tilias, Monte ☎291 782
261. Daily 8am–9pm. Just above
the main bus stop on Largo da
Fonte, this is a fine spot for a
drink or an inexpensive light
meal, including good salads
and superb sandwiches using
homemade bread. The interior is
lined with old prints of Monte and
the disused railway.

Belomonte
Caminho do Monte 184, Monte
☎291 741 444. Mon–Sat 8am–8pm.
Just above the start of the
toboggan run, the top-floor
restaurant here is one of the

best bets for a cooked meal
in Monte, offering reasonably
priced Portuguese dishes and
salads from around €6. The
first-floor café is a popular, if
smoky, retreat for the toboggan
operators.

Café do Monte
Caminho dos Barbosas 8, Monte.
Daily 9am–6pm. Right below the
entrance to the cable car, this
bustling café-restaurant has a
cobbled terrace with sweeping
views. Inside you're spoilt for
choice with very good-value set
lunches, salads and dishes such as
lapas (limpets) with garlic butter.
Also does various drinks, snacks
and pastries.

Xoupana
Choupana Hills, Travessa do Largo
da Choupana, Choupana ☎291
206 020. Daily 7–11pm. Part of
the *Choupana Hills* resort, this
restaurant wins top marks for
style and views, though you'll
need to reserve a table and
expect to pay €30 and upwards
for a full meal. Soaring ceilings
and designer furniture set
the tone, while dishes such as
superb mixed seafood and game
whet the appetite. Unusual
soups, speciality breads and
sumptuous tropical fruit desserts
top it all off.

Northwest of Funchal

Some of Madeira's most spectacular landscapes lie within a short distance of the capital, including the awe-inspiring sea cliffs at Cabo Girão, the world's second highest, and a dizzying sight from above or below. If you're feeling brave enough you can descend the cliff face in a glass-fronted lift to the neighbouring Fajã dos Padres. The cliffs can also be viewed from below at Câmara de Lobos, one of the most traditional fishing villages on the island, whose pretty harbour Winston Churchill often came to paint. Inland, the remote village of Curral das Freiras, set in a valley surrounded by the island's highest peaks, gives a taste of the island's extraordinary mountainous interior.

Câmara de Lobos

Câmara de Lobos, 8km west of Funchal, is one of the island's most atmospheric fishing villages and is heavily promoted as the erstwhile favourite painting spot of Winston Churchill (see box on p.106). Despite the rash of new development on the outskirts, the centre of the village remains instantly likeable and charismatic, with its whitewashed houses, shops and bars. The stony beach doubles as the harbour, filled with colourful beached fishing boats.

The village was named after *lobos de mar* – monk seals ("sea wolves" in Portuguese) – which were frequent visitors to the harbour when it was first settled by Gonçalves Zarco in 1420, and have since become the

▼ CÂMARA DE LOBOS

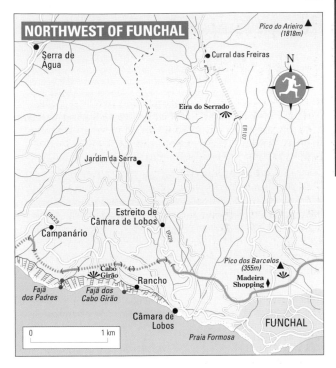

symbol of Madeira. There are
no monk seals here nowadays,
however (they are one of the
most endangered species in the
world, forced to the remoter
shores of the Ilhas Desertas),
and the local fishermen who
hastened their departure
now make their living out of
catching *espada* (scabbard fish).

You can inspect the catch at
the 7am fish market (Mon–Sat),
held in a concrete harbourside
building, an atmospheric affair
that is usually over within
an hour or so, with market
traders repairing to the nearest
bar afterwards. Things are
particularly lively on Sunday
mornings, when off-duty

Visiting Câmara de Lobos

If you have a car, the best approach to Câmara de Lobos is along the old coast road
via the Hotel Zone (20min); a journey of around ten minutes. There are pay-and-
display bays around the harbour and along the through road. Câmara de Lobos is
also served by Rodoeste buses #1, #7 and #27 from Funchal (Mon–Fri 1–2 hourly,
Sat & Sun hourly; 25min). Buses drop you off at **Largo da República**, a little
square in the west end of town above a multistorey car park. The **tourist office** is
on the main Rua São João de Deus 40 (Mon–Fri 9am–12.30pm & 2pm–5pm, Sat
9.30am–noon; ☎ 291 943 470) and can provide information about private *quartos*
(rooms) if you wish to stay the night.

Winston Churchill in Madeira

A plaque to the east of Câmara de Lobos's harbour marks the spot where Winston Churchill liked to sit and paint during his stay on the island in 1950. Before becoming a politician, Churchill worked as a reporter for the *Morning Post* during the Boer War and visited Madeira in October 1899 en route to South Africa. Half a century later, following a heavy defeat in the 1945 general election and a minor stroke in 1949, he decided to return, hoping that the island would be "warm, paintable, bathable, comfortable, flowery" and the ideal place for him to write his memoirs. Churchill stayed at *Reid's* (see p.72), though the suite he was put up in was in a state of disrepair after the war years and ended up being partially furnished by donations from the island's British community. Here he wrote the fourth volume of his war memoirs, *The Hinge of Fate*.

When he wasn't writing, Churchill liked to paint. He travelled to Câmara de Lobos in a grey Rolls-Royce owned by the Leacocks, a wealthy family of wine merchants, who are said to have stuffed the Rolls' boot with drink to "help" him with his painting. Churchill's visit to Madeira was cut short when Clement Attlee declared a new election date, and he returned to Southampton by flying boat in late 1949 to campaign for what proved to be another defeat. He is still remembered fondly on the island, and *Reid's Palace Hotel*'s top room remains the Churchill Suite, much improved from the time he stayed there himself.

fishermen fill the bars with animated conversation and play games of cards on upturned boxes in the harbour.

Nossa Senhora da Conceição and around

Rua Nossa Senhora da Conçeição, Câmara de Lobos. Just back from the harbour, the small but beautiful fishermen's chapel of Nossa Senhora da Conceição is the second oldest on the island, embellished with fifteenth-century pictures depicting scenes of shipwrecks and drownings in the life of St Nicholas, the patron saint of seafarers.

Igreja de São Sebastião

Rua São João de Deus, Câmara de Lobos. Located near the top of Rua São João de Deus – the main drag from the harbour heading west, full of traditional shops and bars – is the Igreja de São Sebastião. Parts of the church date back to the fifteenth century, though in the main it's an eighteenth-century confection, complete with Baroque altar, overbearing chandeliers and a sky-blue ceiling painted with clouds; there are also some attractive azulejos.

Largo da República and the promenade

Just to the west of the rocky bluff that splits Câmara de Lobos into two, Largo da República offers fantastic views

▼ CHURCHILL'S FAVOURITE PAINTING SPOT

over the cliffs of the nearby Cabo Girão. It also marks the start of the sea-facing Rua Nova da Praia, above a modern seafront promenade. Take either, both of which skirt round the bluff, for a breezy walk back to the harbour.

Henrique e Henrique

Estrada de Santa Clara, Câmara de Lobos ☎291 941 551. Mon–Fri 9am–1pm & 2.30–5.30pm. If you want to sample some of the local wine, head up Rua de Santa from Largo da República and you'll see huge barrels in the glass-fronted modern wine lodge, Henrique e Henrique. Dating from 1850, the lodge owns the largest vineyards on the island and produces some of the best Madeira wines around. There are free tastings and all the wines are for sale.

Estreito de Câmara de Lobos and the Levada do Norte

Rodoeste bus #137 (8–15 daily; 1hr). The road from Câmara de Lobos to Cabo Girão winds 10km up through traditionally terraced vineyards to **Estreito de Câmara de Lobos**, the centre of one of Madeira's most important wine-producing areas. The village comes alive during the September Madeira Wine Festival, when the harvest is celebrated with traditional barefoot wine treading and folk dancing. At other times it's a decidedly quiet but a very attractive place, centred on a nineteenth-century church, with far-reaching views over the surrounding valleys. There's also a lively covered market (Mon–Sat), downhill from the central square, Sítio da Igreja.

The village lies close to the **Levada do Norte**– you'll see signs off the main road – which offers some lovely walking opportunities. The *levada* runs north to the Encumeada Pass (see p.145), but the easiest walk from here is south to Quinta Grande (2hr 30min) and Campanário (a further 1hr 30min). The *levada* passes through verdant vineyards, with beautiful views over the coast. If you don't feel like walking the return leg you can

▼ VINEYARDS AROUND ESTREITO DE CÂMARA DE LOBOS

get bus #7 or #107 back from Quinta Grande or Campário to Estreito de Câmara de Lobos.

Cabo Girão

Rodoeste bus #154 stops near the cliffs (Mon–Fri 4 daily, Sat 2 daily; 1hr). The sea cliffs of Cabo Girão are some of the highest in the world, so named because Zarco got this far on his first exploration of Madeira's coast in 1418 before he did an about-turn (*girão*) back to Funchal. There is a small and, thankfully, well-railed lookout point right at the top, from where you can peer straight down the 580m drop to the sea below and across towards the distant Hotel Zone to the east. It's a lovely and tranquil spot, at least when coach parties aren't visiting, with the smell of pine and eucalyptus in the air. There's a small café (Mon–Fri 9am–4pm) opposite the viewpoint, with an adjacent exhibition space displaying art and photographs, usually related to the cliffs.

▼ CABO GIRÃO

Vines and vegetables are cultivated at the foot of the cliffs, which in the past could only be reached by boat or by climbing down the cliffs by rope. Things are a bit easier nowadays thanks to the cable car (Mon 8am–9am & 5–8pm, Tues–Fri 8am–7pm, Sun 9am–7pm, €3) which runs from Rancho, halfway back to Câmara de Lobos. The ride is not for vertigo sufferers, though there's a decent beach at the bottom.

The cliffs are equally impressive from the sea: there are half-day boat tours to the waters below Cabo Girão from Funchal harbour.

Fajã dos Padres

No public transport. West of Cabo Girão is Fajã dos Padres, a tropical fruit farm with its own beachside restaurant in a spectacular location below 300-metre-high cliffs. You can park at the top of the cliff, from where an improbable and somewhat scary lift with glass doors (ring for service; Mon & Wed–Sun 11am–6pm; €8 return per person) rattles down the sheer cliff face. At the foot, a path zig zags down to a pricey café-restaurant, just above a stony beach where the calm waters are great for swimming.

The farm was once part of the vast Quinta Grande estate, originally owned by Zarco's descendants, but gradually sold to the Jesuits, who had acquired the whole estate by 1595. As well as farming the land, the Jesuits used Fajã dos Padres as a retreat, setting up a chapel, which has now been converted into an *adega* (wine lodge). The Jesuits ran the estate until their expulsion in 1759 by the Marquês de Pombal, who was suspicious of the power they wielded, and Fajã dos Padres passed into private hands.

The estate's sheltered position makes it ideal for growing vines, and the warmth radiating from the cliffs is also conducive to the growth of tropical fruits, such as mangoes, papaya, avocado, passion fruit and guavas.

Pico dos Barcelos

Horários do Funchal city bus #9, or #12 from Avenida do Mar, or #4 from Estrada Monumental (every 20–30min; 20–30 min). High above the Hotel Zone, the tree-topped *miradouro* of Pico dos Barcelos enjoys sweeping views over the coast to the south and the impressive twin-spired church of Santo António to the north. If you want to pause longer, there's the handy *Barcelos à Noite* café-restaurant here, too.

Eira do Serrado

São Gonçalo bus #81, 1–3 daily. Many visitors approach Curral das Freiras via the new tunnel, but taking the old road gives you a chance to take in Eira do Serrado, the site of a breathtaking *miradouro*. You can leave your car at the car park, and at the far side of a small

▲ ROAD TO CURRAL DAS FREIRAS, EIRA DO SERRADO

tourist complex, a five-minute climb up steps takes you to a spectacular and hair-raising rock ledge, overlooking Curral das Freiras in the horseshoe-shaped valley of the Ribeira dos Socorridos far below. The valley, whose three sheer sides cut into the serrated peaks of Madeira's highest mountains, was believed for many years to have been a volcanic crater, but it is now known that its dramatic geographical shape was created in large part by the river itself.

Back at the car park, behind the hotel, café and souvenir shop, a cobbled track winds

▲ VIEWPOINT, PICO DOS BARCELOS

There's only one Ronaldo

Head anywhere on Madeira and you will see the face of Cristiano Ronaldo staring at you from posters, the front of T-shirts and virtually any sports paper or magazine – his face has even represented Madeira at EU trade fairs. Considered one of the best footballers in the world, the homegrown star has a hero status unrivalled on the island. Born in Funchal in 1985, Cristiano Ronaldo dos Santos Aveiro gained his nickname from Ronald Reagan, his father's favourite actor. He grew up in a humble house in Santo Antonio, a hilltop district close to Pico dos Barcelos, honing his football skills at amateur local team Andorinha where his father was the kit man. By the time he was nine, Funchal big boys Nacional signed him up for the price of two team kits. His prowess soon alerted mainland giants Sporting and at just eleven he had moved to Lisbon – now for the price of two team kits and a token fee. Sporting nurtured his prodigious pace, fiercesome shots and stepover skills, and despite being initially bullied for his Madeiran accent, he was soon a first-team regular.

In 2003, Manchester United played in a friendly match to inaugurate Sporting's new Alvalade Stadium, and so comprehensively did Ronaldo torment their defence that the United players allegedly asked for him to be signed up – which they duly did, for a fee of over £12 million. Prone to Gazza-like tears in defeat and voted sexiest player of Euro 2004 (admittedly by a Dutch gay magazine), Ronaldo's cult status on Madeira is assured, especially as he keeps strong links with the island. When he first joined United, the chant "There's only one Ronaldo" was a taunt from opposition fans for his supposed inferiority to his better known Brazilian namesake. Now the same words are gleefully chanted by his own fans in the knowledge that he has truly supplanted the former World Footballer of the Year.

steeply down towards Curral das Freiras, an hour's walk away. Though sometimes closed because of landslides, it offers a very beautiful approach to the village – indeed, until 1959, it was the only way there.

Curral das Freiras

São Gonçalo bus #81 from Funchal's Zona Velha (Mon–Fri roughly hourly, Sat & Sun 8 daily; 1hr 15min). Curral das Freiras is one of the most spectacularly situated rural settlements on the island, in a huge natural amphitheatre

surrounded by some of Madeira's highest peaks. The village was founded in the sixteenth century by the nuns of Funchal's Convento de Santa Clara, who fled the capital after a vicious pirate attack in 1566, when around a thousand French pirates looted the island over a period of sixteen days. The nuns sought refuge in a remote valley almost at the centre of the island, which they had traditionally used for farming, and the village that subsequently grew up here became known as the Curral das Freiras, the "Nun's Valley".

Neither the nuns (nor their convent) are around any longer, and today's villagers survive on agriculture and, increasingly, on tourism. Life revolves round the cafés and bars on the small central square, a superb spot, surrounded by a pretty collection of white, shuttered houses overhung with blossom, vines and orange trees.

Next to the square, steps lead down to the attractive town church, Nossa Senhora do Livramento, built in the nineteenth century to replace the crumbling convent. It contains some lovely azulejos, a painted ceiling, and – unusually for Portugal – attractive stained-glass windows.

Head up the side of the *Nun's Valley Restaurante* for lovely views of orange groves and flower-draped houses with little statues of birds and faces on the corners of the roof tiles.

One of the best times to visit is in November, when the village holds the *Festa da Castanha*, a lively chestnut fair.

Shops

Madeira Shopping

Santa Quitéria, St. António ⓦ www .madeirashopping.pt. Shops: Mon–Thurs 10am–11pm, Fri & Sat 10am–midnight. City bus #8, #8A, #16 or #50 from Estrada Monumental. Signed off the road to Pico do Barcelos, this is one of Madeira's largest shopping centres, with 112 national and international shops including Body Shop, Timberland, Mango, Zara, Massimo Dutti and the toy shop Imaginarium. There are also seven cinema screens, and various cafés and restaurants (daily noon–midnight).

▲ CURRAL DAS FREIRAS

Hotels

Estalagem Quinta do Estreito

Rua José Joaquim da Costa, Estreito de Câmara de Lobos ☎ 291 910 530, ⓦ www.charminghotelsmadeira.com. A tastefully converted five-star quinta set in its own sumptuous grounds. The plush rooms are in the quinta's modern extensions and come with cable TV, all mod-cons, verandas and great views over the valleys around. There are also two restaurants, an outdoor pool, sun terrace and sauna, not to mention a lavender field outside for the ultimate feel-good smell. €230.

Restaurants

A Capoeira

Sítio da Igreja, Estreito de Câmara de Lobos. Tues–Sun noon–3.30pm & 6–11pm. Right on the main square with an upstairs room offering unbeatable views across the precipitous valleys below. Vast slabs of meat and kebabs are grilled on metal skewers over a huge fire at the back, along with other Madeiran dishes, at very reasonable prices.

Churchill

Rua João Gonçalves 39, Câmara de Lobos ☏291 941 451. Daily 11am–11pm. Located just above the spot where Churchill liked to paint, this place serves decent, if expensive, Madeiran food, including flambés and seafood platters. You can eat in the cosy wood-lined interior or on the terrace, which is also open for drinks.

Coral

Largo da República, Câmara de Lobos ☏291 942 469. Daily noon–3pm & 6–11pm. Modern café-restaurant on the east side of the main square with a range of tasty, moderately priced grilled meats and fish, plus a superb upstairs terrace affording views over the sea and Cabo Girão.

Nun's Valley Restaurante

Curral das Freiras. Daily 9am–7pm. The most touristy place in the village, but superbly positioned, with a terrace offering sweeping views down the valley. The moderately priced menu includes local specialities such as chestnut soup, banana cake and chestnut cake, while the bar is lined with local liqueurs made from walnuts, passion fruit and chestnuts: you can sample them first before buying. If this place is full, *Nun's Valley II*, just down the hill, serves similar fare.

Peixe na Praia

Praia do Vigário, Câmara de Lobos. ☏291 940 112. Daily 1.30pm–10.30pm. Overlooking the sea, *Peixe na Praia* ("Fish on the Beach") is a friendly place for reasonably priced fresh fish which you can select from the counter. Also does fine vegetarian dishes including a sublime Thai risotto.

Bars

Amarr 'a Boia

Rua Nossa Senhora da Conçeição 8–10, Câmara de Lobos. Daily 9am–midnight. One of the town's liveliest and trendiest bars, with good music, the usual range of local and international drinks and doors at the back opening up to reveal views over the harbour.

A Ginja

Rua da Achada 13, Estreito de Câmara de Lobos. Daily 7am–midnight. A traditional old *adega* with wood beams and walls lined with barrels; head here to sample inexpensive local wines and cider.

Bar No.2 é p'ra Poncha

Largo Poço 1, Câmara de Lobos. Mon–Sat 11am–2am. This bar specializes in Madeira's famous *poncha*, which is usually made from *aguardente* (a local rum), honey and lemon juice, though there are an impressive number of variations on offer here, including *poncha* made with passion fruit, orange, and a particularly lethal one made with absinthe. There's an upstairs room and a downstairs bar, though most people spill out onto the street.

Spatyum

Rua da Carreira 6–8, Câmara de Lobos. Daily 1pm–4am. A lively night spot serving a range of shots, *caipirinha* and *poncha*, which loosens tonsils for regular karaoke sessions. There are also large plasma screens, Internet access, frequent live music and an outdoor terrace for when it all gets too much.

The southeast and Machico

Southeastern Madeira is fairly developed, with two modern package resorts at Garajau and Caniço de Baixo and the more traditional little town of Santa Cruz, which is developing into a resort in its own right thanks to a fine beach, bustling market and water park. Machico, Madeira's second town, set round a pebble and sand beach, is one of the island's most enjoyable and historic places, full of lively cafés and restaurants. Up in the hills, away from the coastal highway, the quiet village of Camacha is famed for its wicker trade.

Garajau

Empresa de Automóveis do Caniço bus #136 (1–2 daily) or #155 (14–16 daily; 20min). Perched on a rocky headland, Garajau is little more than a strip of modern cafés, restaurants, shops and one giant hotel, the *Dom Pedro*. The village gets its name from the *garajaus* – terns – that nest on the cliffs round here, and it's the views from the cliffs that make the place worth a visit.

From the main strip a road forks to the right and winds down the cliff face past pristine new villas to a statue of Christ – a miniature version of those in Rio and Lisbon – more impressive for its location than for any artistic merit. Erected in 1927 on a rocky bluff, it offers fine views of Funchal and of passing tankers heading for the harbour. A cable car (daily; €3 return) links the car park by the statue to a decent stony beach way below at the foot of the cliffs – alternatively you can drive half way down and walk the rest.

Caniço de Baixo

The resort of Caniço de Baixo (Lower Caniço), 2km below the older town of Caniço, is made up of a string of modern villas and hotel complexes built on a low cliff. The western end is the most appealing part of the resort, with a series of low-rise buildings set amongst lush

▼ STATUE OF CHRIST, GARAJAU

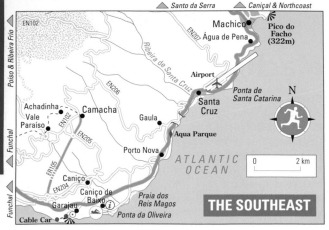

vegetation and leafy gardens just back from the sea. You won't meet many Madeirans here: the resort is something of a German enclave, with German expats running several of the town's facilities.

The pristine waters off the coast are part of the Reserva Natural Parcial do Garajau, a marine reserve which extends from the high tide line to a depth of 50m. The best place to swim or snorkle is at the **Lido Galo Mar** (daily: June–Sept 9am–7pm; Oct–May 10am–6pm; Mon–Fri €3, Sat & Sun €4), reached via a lift, a short walk behind the tourist office. Here, a series of rock and cement sun terraces face a seawater pool and some slippery ladders that you can climb down into the clear blue sea. You can hire out snorkelling equipment from the Manta Diving Centre (see p.197).

Praia dos Reis Magos

East of the Lido Galo Mar, an attractive seafront promenade extends for around 1km past a cluster of modern hotels down the hill to Praia dos Reis Magos, a traditional fishing harbour, with a stony beach and small swimming complex; you can swim here for free and, apart from the stones, conditions are just as good as at the lido. The beach has a much more local feel than the rest of Caniço de Baixo, though it can get crowded in summer.

▲ PICNIC SPOT, GARAJAU

Visiting Caniço de Baixo

Empresa de Automóveis do Caniço bus #155 serves the resort from the Zona Velha in Funchal roughly hourly, taking forty minutes. Buses stop near the **tourist office** (Mon–Fri 9.30am–1pm & 2.30–5.30pm, Sat 9.30am–noon; ☎ 291 932 919), at the top of the village, where there is usually room to park.

Caniço

Empresa de Automóveis do Caniço bus #2, #109 and #155 (Mon–Sat 18 daily, Sun 12 daily; 40min). Set on a hillside 10km east of Funchal, the thriving satellite town of Caniço makes a pleasant stop and is well stocked with restaurants (see p.122). It originally owed its wealth to its position on the divide between Madeira's two "captaincies", or governed districts, and it was for a long time an important agricultural centre. Today the town's most notable feature is its handsome Baroque church, which dominates one side of the attractive central square, Largo Padre Lomelino. Just south of here are the sumptuous botanical gardens attached to the luxury *Quinta Splendida* and open to non-guests, full of exotic flowers and palms.

Camacha

São Gonçalo bus #29 (every 30–60min; 1hr). Set on a hill in the heart of the island's willow plantations some 14km northeast of Funchal, Camacha is the centre of Madeira's money-spinning wicker industry and home to one of the island's largest handicrafts centres, O Relógio (see p.116). In August, the village also displays local handicrafts during its annual arts fair.

The centre of the village is dominated by the Largo da Achada, a cobbled square the size of a football pitch – probably because it used to be one. It is said that Harry

▼ CHURCH SQUARE, CANIÇO

The wicker trade

Though wicker baskets had long been made in Madeira, the craft didn't take off until the nineteenth century, when the same Hinton family that brought soccer to Madeira managed to persuade local farmers to diversify into wicker-weaving so as not to be over-reliant on the wine trade. There was soon a healthy demand for wicker – especially cane furniture – in Britain's former colonies. The industry has slumped somewhat since then, but better production techniques have helped craftsmen to make a wider range of products, and tourist demand keeps around two thousand workers employed in and around Camacha.

Wicker comes from willows, which thrive in the damp ground around Camacha. The larger branches of the trees are used like conventional wood, while the narrower, flexible branches are harvested in spring, then soaked, stripped of bark and dried to form wicker. Depending on the length of the branches, the wicker is then woven into baskets, furniture or other products.

Hinton, a member of the wealthy Hinton family, who once owned the Ilhas Desertas, brought a football back from a trip to England, which led to Portugal's first ever game of soccer being played out on Camacha's main square in 1875 – an event commemorated on a plaque to one side of the square.

A sign on the square points to the Levada dos Tornos (see p.101), which continues all the way to Quinta do Palheiro Ferreiro (around two hours' walk away) and beyond. To the north of the square, the Portela road heads uphill past the post office to the village's old church, a slightly run-down-looking Baroque building that seems to

have been neglected in favour of the ungainly modern church below the main square, whose thunderous chimes ring out every quarter of an hour.

O Relógio

Camacha's main square, Largo do Achada, is loomed over by the white O Relógio building, the tourist nerve centre of the whole village. Once the home of a British merchant's family, it was named after the *relógio* (clock) brought to Madeira from the parish church of Woolton near Liverpool by local doctor Michael Grabham in 1896. Though the distinctive nineteenth-century clocktower still exists, the building has been considerably altered, and today consists of a hotel, café, restaurant (see p.124) and shop (see p.122). It also hosts the island's most famous folk group, the Grupo Folclorico da Casa do Povo da Camacha, who play in the restaurant every Friday and Saturday night at 9.15pm (unless away on tour).

Santa Cruz

SAM bus #53 or #156 (6–12 daily; 50min). Despite its proximity to

▼ SANTA CRUZ

both the coastal highway and the airport, Santa Cruz is a very appealing place – well worth a detour or even an overnight stay on your first or last night on Madeira. The town has a lovely palm-lined seafront, a fine nineteenth-century courthouse and attractive Igreja de Santa Cruz, one of the oldest and best preserved churches on Madeira, with its original sixteenth-century Manueline touches preserved intact. From the church, Rua Conégo César de Oliveira leads down to Praceta, a small square where elderly men hang out on benches under leafy trees and arbours.

The lido and seafront

The eastern part of Santa Cruz's seafront is taken up by a lido, Praia das Palmeiras (daily 9am–7pm; ☎291 524 248; free), with a seawater pool and a separate kids' pool opposite the town jetty. Next to the lido on Rua da Praia, you'll also find the small covered market (Mon & Sat 7am–4pm, Tues–Thurs 7am–5pm, Fri 7am–7pm, Sun 7am–1pm), one of the best on the island for fish, and selling every imaginable fruit and vegetable.

The town beach stretches west from the lido, a long swathe of pebbles dotted with little palm shades and backed by palm trees, cafés and a big children's play area; when the sea's calm you can swim out to offshore bathing platforms.

Aqua Parque

Ribeira da Boaventura ☎291 524 412, ⓦwww.aquaparque.com. Daily 10am–6pm, €6.5, children under 12 €4. Just west of Santa Cruz, signed "São Pedro" off the main highway, lies an aquapark,

▲ SANTA CRUZ MARKET

complete with multicoloured slides, flumes and pools. It also lays on summer concerts. You can walk up the seafront promenade from Santa Cruz in about ten minutes.

Madeira airport

Though an odd tourist attraction, Madeira airport really is special, as most visitors to the island find out. Opened in 1964, it was known as the "aircraft carrier" because of its incredibly short runway wedged on a hillside right by the Atlantic, and was considered one of the world's most dangerous places to land. Thankfully, an extension opened in 2000 and now planes touch down on a spacious runway built on stilts over the sea – the coast road passes underneath. Landing can still be a hairy experience, and in certain weather conditions planes are diverted to Porto Santo or, very occasionally, the Canaries. Madeirans are very proud of their airport, and you'll find postcards of various stages in its development all over the island.

▲ MACHICO

Machico

Madeira's second town, Machico, lies just ten minutes' drive east of the airport in a beautiful natural bay surrounded by steep, terraced slopes and fronted by its own stony beach. Though little more than an overgrown village, its laid-back atmosphere, restaurants and modicum of nightlife make it a great base for a holiday, or at least a night or two's stopover.

The focus of town is Largo Dr António Jardim d'Oliveira, the cobbled main square, where taxi drivers chat by their yellow cars in the shade of tall oak trees. The north of the square is taken up by the fifteenth-century

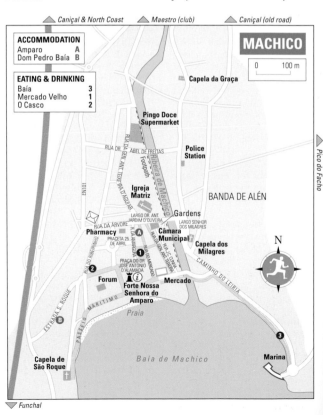

Caniçal & North Coast   Maestro (club)   Caniçal (old road)

MACHICO

0   100 m

ACCOMMODATION
Amparo   A
Dom Pedro Baía B

EATING & DRINKING
Baía   3
Mercado Velho   1
O Casco   2

Capela da Graça

Pingo Doce Supermarket

RUA DR. GEN. ANT. TEIXEIRA D'AGUIAR

RUA DA GEN. ABEL DE FREITAS

Footpath

Police Station

Ribeira de Machico

EN101

Igreja Matriz

BANDA DE ALÉN

LARGO DR. ANT. JARDIM D'OLIVEIRA

Gardens

LARGO SENHOR DOS MILAGRES

RUA DA ÁRVORE

Pharmacy

PRACETA 25 DE ABRIL

R. DA AMARGURA

RUA DA GEN. ANT. TEIXEIRA

Câmara Municipal

Capela dos Milagres

RUA DO REGEADO

PRAÇA DO DR JOSÉ ANTONIO D'ALMADA

CAMINHO DO LEIRIA

N

RUA DO RIBEIRINHO

Forum

Mercado

ESTRADA S. ROQUE

Forte Nossa Senhora do Amparo

PASSEIO MARÍTIMO

Praia

Capela de São Roque

Baía de Machico

Marina

Pico do Facho

Funchal

Visiting Machico

There are various buses to Machico from Funchal; the best services are the SAM bus Machico espresso (Mon–Fri roughly hourly; 55min) and bus #156 (6–14 daily; 1hr) from Rua Calouste Gulbenkian in Funchal. Buses stop at the main square, a short walk to the tourist office in the Forte do Amparo (Mon–Fri 9am–12.30pm & 2–5pm, Sat 9.30am–noon; ☎291 962 289).

Igreja Matriz, built under the orders of Tristão Vaz Teixeira's wife, Branco. Its most distinctive feature is a gracefully arched Manueline door, with three small marble columns.

East of the narrow Ribeira do Machico is an area of old fishermen's houses known as Banda de Alén, centred on the Largo Senhor dos Milagres, a quiet square where old men play cards beneath shady trees. On the southern side of the square stands the simple, whitewashed Capela dos Milagres (Chapel of Miracles). Built in 1815, it replaced an earlier chapel said to have been constructed on the site where Anne d'Arfet (and possibly Robert Machin) was buried (see box on p.120). This was destroyed by a flood in 1803, but miraculously a wooden crucifix survived (having been swept out to sea, it was rescued by a passing ship). The "miraculous" recovery of the crucifix is still celebrated every October 8 with a torchlit procession and a local public holiday on the following day.

Machico's seafront

Machico's beach, backed by a modern seafront promenade, is the focus of the town in summer. At low tide the sea withdraws to reveal a narrow sandy stretch, onto which everyone descends to avoid walking on the large, steeply banked pebbles behind. The water in the bay isn't the cleanest, though its brown colour is caused by the mud sea bed rather than anything more unpleasant, and there are usually sunloungers and umbrellas for hire.

Fronting the beach is the Forte Nossa Senhora do Amparo, a low, pale-yellow fort built in 1706 to protect the town against pirate attack. Passing pirates were a permanent menace to the local population, and Machico's forts were built so that soldiers could hole up after the women and children had retreated inland.

▲ PROMENADE, MACHICO

PLACES | The southeast and Machico

▲ DIVING OFF MACHICO

Nowadays the fort houses the tourist office (see box on p.119).

The west of the promenade ends below the Capela de São Roque, built in 1739 as a token of gratitude to the eponymous saint for saving the town from the plague. Unfortunately, it's normally locked, but if you do manage to get in you'll see some beautiful eighteenth-century azulejos showing São Roque, who dedicated his life to helping plague victims.

On the opposite side of the bay, by the marina, a jetty marks the spot at which the first Portuguese set foot on Madeira: a sign reads "Tristão Vaz Teixeira and João Goncalves Zarco disembarked here on 2 July, 1419".

Pico do Facho

The eastern side of Machico's bay is loomed over by Pico do Facho, a 320-metre-high peak named after the beacon (*facho*)

A brief history of Machico

Legend has it that Machico's name derives from Robert Machin, an English merchant who eloped from Bristol with his wealthy lover Anne d'Arfet in 1346. Heading for Spain, their boat was thrown off course and blown against the rocks off Machico, and, although they managed to swim ashore with other members of the crew, Anne later became ill and died. Some versions of the legend say Machin also died here, others that the broken-hearted Machin buried Anne before he managed to escape from the island on a raft, following which he was captured by pirates and sold as a slave in Morocco. Here, Machin apparently related his woes to a Spanish slave, who, on returning to Iberia, spread Machin's tale. News of the Atlantic island eventually reached the Portuguese court, inspiring Zarco to search for Madeira. When he first landed on the island, Zarco was said to have found Anne's grave, leading him to name the place after Machin. A less romantic explanation is that Machico is named after Monchique, Zarco's home town in Portugal.

Either way, Machico was the first spot on the island to be colonized and was Madeira's capital from 1440 to 1496 under Tristão Vaz Teixeira, whose statue now stands in the main square. When the island was unified in 1497, the capital moved to Funchal, and Machico became a centre for sugar production and fishing.

that used to be lit here to warn residents of approaching pirates. The tradition of lighting a beacon is resurrected on the last Sunday of August, when a large bonfire is lit here to celebrate the Festa do Santíssimo Sacramento.

With a car, you can reach the top by driving out of town for around 2km on the old road towards Caniçal and turning right 200m or so after the *Restaurante Típico O Túnel* (if you pass through a tunnel you've gone too far) onto a side road signed Pico do Facho. Continue up the road until the tarmac runs out and becomes a dirt track; you can walk the remaining 1km to the peak.

Hotels

Alpino Atlantico

Rua Robert Baden Powell, Caniço de Baixo ☎ 291 930 930, ⊛ www .galoresort.com. Tucked away in a leafy side street, this is a relatively small hotel and all the better for it, with just 24 spacious doubles, most with sea-facing balconies, and a small swimming pool. €122.

Residencial Amparo

Rua da Amargura, Machico ☎ 291 968 120 or ☎ 964 523 853. A modern, friendly *residencial* built in traditional style, close to the seafront. The twelve rooms are on the small side, but they are pristine and come with en-suite bathrooms and cable TV. €45.

Dom Pedro Baía

Estrada de São Roque, Machico ☎ 291 969 500, ⊛ www.dompedro .com. Machico's only high-rise building dominates the west side of the beach. The main block has reasonably sized rooms with

good views over the bay, though no balconies – unlike those in the low-rise annexe next door. The four-star facilities include a seawater pool in the small grounds, tennis, a fairly poor in-house restaurant and access to watersports facilities and diving (see p.197). €75.

Dom Pedro Garajau

Estrada do Garajau 131, Garajau ☎ 291 930 800, ⊛ www.dompedro.com. This giant, rather anonymous three-star hotel takes up one entire side of the road into Garajau. Out of the three hundred-odd rooms, those at the top of blocks 1 and 2 have the best views. There are also studios with tiny kitchenettes for self-catering, though standard double rooms are slightly larger. Facilities include a pool, table tennis and restaurant, and nightly entertainment programme. €85.

Inn & Art

Rua Robert Baden Powell 61–62, Caniço de Baixo ☎ 291 938 200, ⊛ www.innart.com. German-run restaurant and hotel offering a mixed bag of rooms, some of which are in a separate annexe up the hill with a small plunge pool – the best ones have great sea views. There are a range of tariffs and car rental options, with prices starting at €120 for a double room (with breakfast) or an apartment (without breakfast). One week minimum stay in high season.

Quinta Splendida Wellness

Estrada da Ponta da Oliveira, Caniço ☎ 291 930 400, ⊛ www .hotelquintasplendida.com. Impressive hotel and spa complex with a mix of rooms and apartments – with kitchenette and balcony – set round beautifully landscaped botanical gardens; most also have sea views, though you pay extra for this. There are two restaurants, two bars (one by the pool), a nightly entertainment programme, a spa and fitness centre and outdoor swimming pool. Double rooms from €110, double apartments from €125.

Residencial Santo António

Rua Cónego César de Oliveira, Santa Cruz ☎ 291 524 198, ☎ 291 524 264. An attractive guesthouse on the main drag between the beach and church. Azulejos-lined corridors lead to large, clean rooms, each with their own bathroom, TV and either a balcony or terrace. €7 extra for breakfast. €35.

Vila Ventura

Caminho Cais da Oliveira, Caniço de Baixo ☎ 291 934 611, ⓦ www .villa-ventura.com. A relatively small hotel by Caniço de Baixo standards, with 22 spacious studios, each with satellite TV, bath and balcony – though any sea views are partially blocked by the *Tropical Hotel* opposite. Facilities include a bar and garden restaurant, and staff also rent out mountain bikes and arrange walks. Breakfast costs €10 extra. €60.

Shops

O Relógio

Largo do Achada, Camacha. Daily 9.30am–8.30pm. A giant emporium best known for its wicker (see box on p.116). Just about anything that can be made out of wicker is sold here: baskets, chairs, umbrella stands, shelving units, toys, plant holders, trays and hats. Bigger items are to be found on level 1, including a giant wicker boat and a menagerie of wicker animals, among them a ten-foot giraffe. If you find such quirky objects irresistible, they can be delivered abroad. You can watch the stuff being made in the workshop on level 2. The shops also sells various souvenirs including ceramics, azulejos tiles, liqueurs, Madeira wine and rugs.

Cafés

Esplanada Alameda

Rua da Praia, Santa Cruz. Daily 7am–1am. This attractive café with wrought-iron chairs and marble table tops sits on the seaside promenade beneath palms and facing the colourful beached fishing boats. It offers the usual range of drinks, snacks and pastries including great croissants and fresh juices.

Restaurants

Atlantis

Lido Galo Mar, Caniço de Baixo ☎ 291 930 930. Daily noon–10pm. Set on a terrace overlooking the sea and pool, this lido restaurant offers top service, fine buffet lunches and unusual evening meals such as *lombo de espadarte em casca de eucalipto* (swordfish roasted in eucalyptus bark), couscous dishes and *cataplana* stews. Mains around €10.

Bilheteira

Praça Dr João Abel de Freitas 11, Santa Cruz ☎ 291 522 124. Daily 11am–11pm. There's a refreshingly long menu of very reasonably priced fish and meats at this cosy modern place with outdoor tables facing Santa Cruz's main church. Great tuna or salmon from around €6.

▲ O CASCO

O Boleo

Sítio da Igreja, Camacha ☎ 291 922 128. Daily noon–3pm & 7–11pm. This place has a big outdoor barbecue and specializes in sizzling grilled meat dishes and *frango no churrasco* (barbecue-grilled chicken). There are tables inside and out and a list of daily specials such as stewed tongue. Full meals for around €15.

O Casco

Rua do Ribeirinho, Machico ☎ 291 962 150. Daily noon–11pm; bar open until 2am. With palm-frond sun-umbrellas and an outdoor patio, this is the best place in Machico for a good, no-nonsense, filling meal for under €15. Service is friendly, and there's a fine bar area where you can hole up inside giant wine barrels.

Inn and Art

Rua Robert Baden Powell 61–62, Caniço de Baixo ☎ 291 938 200. Daily noon–3pm & 6–10.30pm. An arty restaurant, just west of the tourist office, with modern paintings on the walls by German artist Siegward Sprotte, though most people head for the sea-facing terrace on a clifftop. The menu features light, moderately priced lunches and expensive full evening meals with dishes including fish, risotto and "chicken stew sweet and sour". There's usually a nightly live music programme, which ranges from fado to Brazilian.

Mercado Velho

Rua do Mercado, Machico ☎ 291 965 926. Daily 10am–10pm. This former small covered market building opposite the tourist office has been nicely converted into an attractive café-restaurant offering the usual Madeiran favourites, omelettes, salads and a few spaghetti dishes from around €9. The food is nothing special, but the setting – with seats outside on a cobbled terrace complete with a fountain and a few azulejos – is a cut above the rest.

Praia das Palmeiras

Praia das Palmeiras, Santa Cruz ☎ 291 524 248. Daily 9am–10pm, bar open until 11pm. This lido café-restaurant has a great sea-facing terrace and good café snacks such as *rissois de bacalhau*. Full meals include a long list of meat, fish, seafood, salads, omelettes, pasta dishes and the speciality steak. Mains from €9.

O Relógio

Largo da Achada, Camacha. ☏291 922 777. Daily noon–4pm & 7–11pm. Despite the tourist trappings, this is the best place to eat in Camacha, mainly thanks to its unbroken views over the south coast. It can seem quiet when the tour parties aren't filling up its ample spaces, but the food and service is top-notch. The moderately priced dishes include spaghetti, steaks and a mean range of desserts, including chocolate mousse. On Fridays and Saturdays at 9.15pm, the excellent Grupo Folclorico da Casa do Povo da Camacha (see p.116) will compete with the views for your attention.

La Terraça

Rua João Paulo III 30, Caniço ☏291 933 898. Daily noon–3pm & 6–11pm. Head uphill past the church and bag a seat on the terrace of this restaurant, with great views over the coast and the Ilhas Desertas. The menu is quite meaty, with a few fish dishes, including *bacalhau*, from around €9.

O Túnel

Estrada do Caniçal, near Machico ☏291 962 459. Daily 11am–10pm. Located just before the tunnel on the old road to Caniçal, a couple of kilometres out of Machico, this is a reasonably priced place – as long as you avoid the lobster or grilled prawns – with fine grills and outdoor tables offering great views down over the Machico valley. A handy stop-off on the walk from Lorano (see p.132).

Vista Mar

Estrada Garajau, Garajau ☏291 934 110. Daily noon–3pm & 6–10.30pm. Just out of Garajau on the clifftop road to Caniço, this place does indeed have a sea view (*vista mar*) from its tiny dining room, which offers the usual range of well-prepared meat and fish dishes, salads and omelettes from around €7, as well as crepes, and a fine *pudim de maracujá* (passion fruit dessert).

Bars

Baía

Porto de Recreio, Machico. Daily 9am–2am. Ultra-popular bar-restaurant overlooking the marina at the eastern end of Machico. Along with beers, spirits, *poncha* and *caipirinhas* you can enjoy moderately priced seafood facing the water – though on Friday to Sunday nights, everyone piles indoors when karaoke sessions get under way.

Clubs

Maestro

Rua Nova de Graça, Machico ☏291 964 369, ⓦwww.maestrobar.com. Fri–Sun 10pm–1am. This sleek club is short on space but big on atmosphere, with special theme nights, karaoke sessions on Friday and Saturday and ladies night (with three free drinks for the girls) on Friday and Sunday. It's north of the Pingo Doce supermarket opposite the secondary school.

Rock's Club

Caniço Shopping Centre Loja 30, Estrada João Gonçalves Zarco, Caniço ☏291 934 090. Daily 2pm–3am. Despite its location in a shopping centre, this bar/club really does rock, though it's somewhat schizophrenic, with bowling and billiards by day, disco by night. The Wednesday to Sunday club has a resident DJ, hosts live bands and has weekend karaoke sessions.

The east and Porto da Cruz

The east of Madeira is a diverse, wild landscape offering some of the best walks on the island. You can hike the length of the precipitous and craggy headland of Ponta de São Lourenço, where you'll find Madeira's only naturally sandy beach at Prainha. The gateway to the headland, Caniçal was once the centre of a major whaling industry, now remembered in a fascinating museum. Inland, the island's top golf course at Santo da Serra is spectacularly sited, next to a village with a lovely park. North of here lies Porto da Cruz, one of the most picturesque villages on the dramatic north coast.

Caniçal

SAM bus #113 (Mon–Fri 18 daily, Sat & Sun 8–10 daily; 90min). Although Caniçal is easily reached via a new highway from Machico, it's more fun to take the old road, bored through Pico do Facho in 1956. Before then the village could only be reached by boat or by hiking up over the peak. This remoteness made it the ideal site for the main processing plant of the odorous whaling industry, which set up here in 1949. Today Caniçal remains a pretty but earthy fishing village spread along a pebbly beach.

Just above the beach is the main square, where yellow taxis line up alongside the squat town church and the densely packed cemetery. At the western end of the beach you can swim in the Complexo Balnear (€1), which also has its own café-restaurant – a more attractive option than the eastern end of the beach, where the Zona Franca industrial complex houses factories and Madeira's main container port.

Museu da Baleia

Tues–Sun 10am–noon & 1–6pm. €2.50. Caniçal is best known for its Museu da Baleia, set just back from the harbour, tracing the village's whaling industry

▲ FISHERMEN, CANIÇAL

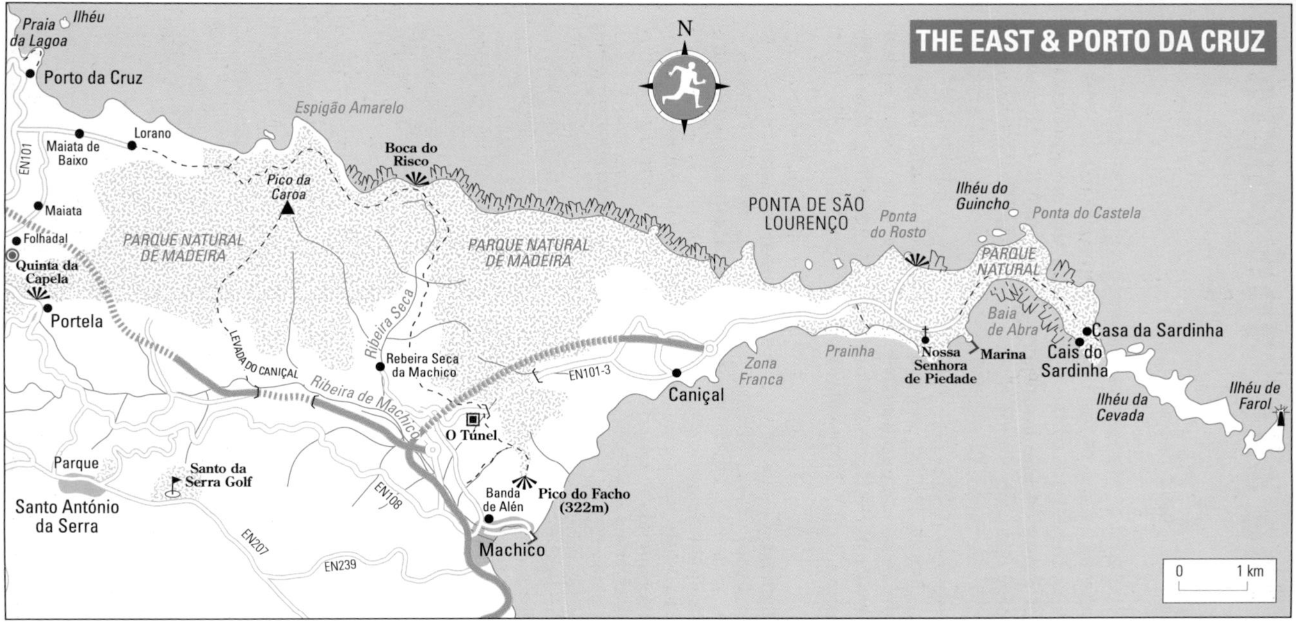

THE EAST & PORTO DA CRUZ

N

0   1 km

Ilhéu de Farol

Ilhéu da Cevada

Casa da Sardinha

Cais do Sardinha

Baía de Abra

Marina

Nossa Senhora de Piedade

Ilhéu do Guincho

Ponta do Castela

PARQUE NATURAL

Ponta do Rosto

PONTA DE SÃO LOURENÇO

Prainha

Zona Franca

Caniçal

Espigão Amarelo

PARQUE NATURAL DE MADEIRA

Boca do Risco

EN101-3

Pico do Facho (322m)

Banda de Além

Machico

O Túnel

Ribeira Seca da Machico

Ribeira Seca

Ribeira de Machico

EN108

EN239

Pico da Caroa

LEVADA DO CANIÇAL

PARQUE NATURAL DE MADEIRA

Santo da Serra Golf

EN207

Lorano

Maiata de Baixo

Maiata

Folhadal

Quinta da Capela

Portela

EN101

Praia do Ilhéu da Lagoa

Porto da Cruz

Parque

Santo António da Serra

– there are plans to move the museum to a new seafront site by late 2008. Whaling thrived in Caniçal until 1981, and the village was even used as one of the locations for John Huston's *Moby Dick* in 1956. To research the film, Huston and Gregory Peck joined the local fleet on a whale hunt, witnessing the death of some twenty animals, a fair proportion of the 250 whales – mostly sperm – that used to be killed annually off Madeiran waters. In 1981, an international moratorium ended whaling in these parts, and the coastal area off Caniçal became a marine reserve in 1986. The tiny museum squeezes in maps and examples of scrimshaw carved into boats, walking sticks and model mermaids. There's a real whaling boat, roughly the length of the model thirteen-metre-long adolescent sperm whale alongside, while the 16.5-metre-long lower-jaw bone of an adult sperm whale gives some idea of their size. There are also details of schemes to protect sperm, fin, humpback and blue whales that cruise past Madeiran waters today, along with other threatened marine species such as dolphins and the rare monk seal. Be warned that the gory video footage of whale processing and photos of kills may be upsetting to some children.

Prainha beach

A couple of kilometres east of Caniçal – and usually marked by a cluster of parked cars – steps lead down the cliff to the beach at Prainha, which, unusually for Madeira, boasts wonderfully soft, dark-grey sand. The swimming off the beach is also superb, with crystalline water. Not surprisingly, all this attracts a fair few day-trippers, especially at weekends in the summer, so space on the sands can be limited. However, you can always retreat to the terrace of the beachside café (summer only daily 10am–8pm; closed when the weather is bad), where you can get slightly pricey fish and seafood, snacks and drinks; the place also hires out sun beds and umbrellas.

Above the beach is the chapel of Nossa Senhora de Piedade, which comes to life on the third

▲ WHALING BOAT, MUSEU DA BALEIRA

PLACES The east and Porto da Cruz

▲ PONTA DE SÃO LOURENÇO

Sunday of September when a statue of Nossa Senhora de Piedade – attributed by some to an unnamed sixteenth-century Flemish master – is taken from the chapel to Caniçal accompanied by a procession of fishing boats; at other times, the chapel remains locked.

Ponta de São Lourenço

Madeira's craggy easternmost tip, Ponta de São Lourenço, has a very different feel to the rest of the island, at once exposed and barren, the spinning wind turbines at its southwestern end giving it a slightly eerie air. At Ponta do Rosto, there's a small *miradouro* with picnic tables facing dramatic cliffs. After another kilometre, the road ends at a little car park – often occupied by a van selling snacks and cold drinks. Here people stop to admire the views over the sheer drops – some up to 180m high – round the Baia de Abra; you can also see the offshore islets of Ilhéu da Cevada and the lighthouse-topped Ilhéu de Farol. The geography of the landscape

here is more like that of Porto Santo and the Ilhas Desertas than the rest of Madeira, and the vegetation is also distinctive, consisting of cacti, thistles and the red-tipped, seaweed-like ice plants.

Just above the car park, picnic tables offer superb views towards the rock arch at the far end of the headland, though there's little shade and you'll find yourself in lizard territory – sit still enough and the reptiles will crawl up your leg and into your picnic.

The car park also marks the starting point of a footpath which takes you into the Parque Natural de Ponta de São Lourenço right to the tip of the headland, an exhilarating and, at times, vertiginous, three-hour return walk (see below).

The Ponta de São Lourenço walk

The walk from the Baia de Abra car park to the tip of the headland and back (3hr round-trip) is one of the most dramatic on Madeira. The route follows a well-worn path, much of it over bare rock, clearly marked with stones, cairns, white posts or green arrows. Parts of the walk involve fairly steep scrambles over loose scree, and it can be extremely slippery when wet, so make sure you have good footwear. In winter, high winds can also make the walk hazardous, though the steepest parts of the walk have good fences for protection.

Start off heading east from the car park and you quickly pass a sign announcing entry into the Parque Natural. After five minutes, the path divides, with a faint downward fork leading to a lovely stony beach. The left-hand fork goes up to a viewpoint with great views over the north coast and huge cliffs falling into the sea. Continue on this path and after about half an hour from the start you cross bare rock, a fairly steep route. The path then goes over a narrow pass with views over the headland.

Around ten minutes later, you reach the steepest section, with wire fencing on one side leading you down to a very narrow neck of the headland with sheer drops, especially to the north side. The path then crosses fields lined with thistles.

After about 75 minutes into the walk, you'll reach the ranger's house, Casa da Sardinha. From here, you could detour southwest to the coast; a ten-minute walk brings you to a small jetty, Cais do Sardinha, where you can swim if the sea is not too rough.

Back at the ranger's house, allow another seventy-five

▼ PONTA DE SÃO LOURENÇO WALK

minutes to return the way you came.

Santo António da Serra

SAM bus #20 or #78 (Mon–Fri 6 daily, Sat & Sun 2 daily; 1hr 45min); also São Gonçalo bus #77 (5–7 daily; 1hr). The small and unassuming hillside village of Santo António da Serra (AKA Santo da Serra) – is home to one of the island's most famous golf courses, the dramatically sited **Clube de Golf Santo da Serra** (☎291 550 100, ⓦwww.santodaserragolf.com), 1.5km southeast of the village on the EN207. Designed by Robert Trent Jones, the 27-hole course hosts the Madeira Open, usually in February or March, attracting international stars. At a height of 670m, the air is cool here, and at times clouds float between the golf course and the coast below; if you are unlucky the whole place will be swathed in low cloud. Even if you're not a fan of golf, it's worth sneaking into the club house for a drink to admire the stunning views, encompassing the whole of the eastern tip of the island and out to the Ilhas Desertas.

Amid the green woodland between the village and the golf course lie flash quintas and villas, belonging to wealthy Madeirans and expats who have built summer homes here from the eighteenth century onwards. Otherwise, the village itself doesn't have an awful lot going for it. Buses stop in front of the nineteenth-century church; the church once housed an important Flemish work of art, nearly used by the local priest as a wedge to help a passing motorist who had got stuck in mud here in the 1930s. When, by chance, it was discovered how precious the "board" was, the rest of Madeira was scoured for similar works of art, leading to the collection in Funchal's Museu de Arte Sacra (see p.58).

Parque do Santo da Serra

Santo António da Serra's extensive Parque do Santo da Serra is great for families and plant lovers or just for a picnic stop. Wooden gates mark the entrance, from where a cobbled track, lined with agapanthus, camellias and hydrangeas,

▼ CLUBE DE GOLF SANTO DA SERRA

leads down into extensive woodlands. The grounds were once part of an estate owned by the Blandy family, and you can still see the family's pink quinta, now a government office, as you enter the park on your left. For children, there's a nature trail to follow – in Portuguese, but largely pictorial – and a play area next to deer and bird enclosures. There are also tennis courts and a crazy golf course. The path eventually winds down under pine and eucalyptus trees to a

▲ PORTELA PLANT STALL

viewpoint where you can watch clouds scud up from the valley above the distant Ponta de São Lourenço.

Portela

SAM bus #53 (Mon–Fri 3–5 daily, Sat & Sun 1–3 daily; 50min). From Machico, a tunnel slices through the mountains to the north coast, but it's worth taking the slower old road to Porto da Cruz via the dramatic mountain pass of Portela (622m), offering dazzling views over the north coast, here dominated by the giant cube-shaped rock of Penha de Águia (see p.169). The highest point of the pass is marked by stalls selling plants or souvenirs, along with a taxi or two waiting for walkers from Ribeira Frio (see p.169). You'll also find the good *Miradouro da Portela* restaurant here (see p.134).

Porto da Cruz

SAM bus #53 and #78 (Mon–Fri 4 daily, Sat 3 daily, Sun 1 daily; 1hr 10min). One of the most spectacularly sited fishing villages on the north coast, Porto da Cruz is also one of the liveliest, as well as being a good starting point for the dramatic coastal path that goes via Lorano across to Machico. The village's most prominent building is a massive modern church, a ghastly structure with one external wall lined with statues of saints. But if you take the steps below the church to the harbour, you'll be rewarded with stunning views – on one side is the towering rock of Penha de Águia and on the other the steep cliffs and terraced slopes of Pico da Coroa.

The harbour is fronted by a beach made up of giant boulders and backed by a small promenade. Most people head to the west end of the promenade, where there's a superb large seawater swimming pool, complete with a special children's area and café.

The promenade continues west round a grassy knoll to

▲ PORTA DA CRUZ SEA POOL

another stony beach, Praia da Lagoa. It's a pleasant ten-minute stroll, past a little fishing harbour and over a sea cave, which spews spray and rumbles dramatically in high seas. Praia da Lagoa is backed by a big sea terrace, with changing rooms, a café and sunbathing areas. Alongside, with its distinctive brick chimney, is the Companhia dos Engenhos do Norte, a rum distillery – you can peer inside at the ancient machinery and giant wooden barrels, mostly containing the local *aguardente* firewater.

The coastal path from Lorano to Machico

Before the road over the mountains was built, the three-to four-hour walk along the coastal path from Lorano to Machico was the main route east. The path, which skirts the north coast's dramatic cliffs before a gentle descent to Machico, is at times precipitous and also passes through fairly dense areas of bramble, so be sure to wear trousers and walking boots. In addition, before heading off check

locally on the latest conditions along the track, as rock falls have made sections of the walk unsafe.

From Porto da Cruz, it is a tough climb to **Lorano**, some 3km up the coast to the east, so it's probably best to take a taxi straight to the village. Signed Maiata de Baixo off the main Machico road, Lorano is a small hamlet on either side of a dirt track. Continue along the track until it narrows into a path, after about twenty minutes' walk. A little further on the path splits; make sure you take the stonier upper path, which climbs steeply at first. Behind you are great views back towards Porto da Cruz.

After about an hour from the start, you round a headland and suddenly see Ponta da São Lourenço. For the next twenty minutes, the scenery changes dramatically, the dense undergrowth giving way to barren, exposed rock as you skirt the edge of a concave cliff. Watch your footing, especially when it's wet. Shortly after you leave the cliff, the scenery changes again as the path plunges through bracken and broom heather.

Around twenty minutes later, you emerge onto a grassy mountainside and reach the pass of **Boca do Risco** (the Risky Mouth) – so-called because when gales blow, the wind funnels through the pass, and crossing it can be risky indeed. Climb a small path to the right and you'll find a relatively flat grassy picnic spot.

Over the pass, the path descends into a wooded valley of pines and, some half an hour from Boca do Risco, meets a tiny *levada*. Follow the *levada* to the left, and you'll look down on the village of Ribeira Seca do Machico, with its ramshackle, illegally built houses, and within twenty minutes you'll join the old Machico–Canaiçal road.

Turn left and you can continue to Pico do Facho (20–30min). Alternatively, turn right and it's a minute's walk to *O Túnel* restaurant, from where you can call a taxi to Machico (around €7), or continue down the road (30min).

Hotels

Costa Linda

Rua Dr João Abel de Freitas, Porto da Cruz ☎291 560 080, ⊛www .costa-linda.net. Right on the seafront, and built in traditional stone, this modern hotel is tastefully simple, with neutral decor and bright, fresh rooms, most with sea-facing balconies. €50; apartment for two with kitchen for €65.

Estalagem A Quinta

Casais Próximas, Santo António da Serra ☎291 550 030, ⊛www .estalagemaquinta.com. Just north of the centre of town on the Funchal–Portela road, this small, friendly four-star offers decent modern rooms with private bathrooms, TV and a small communal garden. There's also a games room, unheated pool and a moderately priced, rustic-style restaurant (daily noon–11pm), offering the usual range of meat and fish dishes, served inside or on a small covered terrace. €60.

Quinta da Capela

Sítio do Folhado, off the Porto da Cruz–Portela road ☎291 562 491, ⊛www.madeirarural.com. This is serious get-away-from-it-all stuff, on a breezy hillside some 3.5km above Porto da Cruz. Set in a beautiful seventeenth-century quinta (manor house) and chapel reached by steep steps up from the road, the building has national heritage status and is furnished with period pieces, including traditional kitchen implements. The quinta has five spacious and traditionally furnished rooms (though the bathrooms are modern) and its own gardens, from where you can watch buzzards swooping below you towards the coast. But, unless you have the legs of a donkey, a car is essential. €70.

Hotel do Santo

Sítio dos Casais Próximos, Santo António da Serra ☎291 550 550, ⊛www.enotel.com. Four-star splendour just south of the park and ten minutes' walk from the golf course – golfers make up a fair share of the hotel's clients. Spacious rooms are done out in rustic decor and come with satellite TV; most open onto sumptuous lawns. There's also an indoor pool, tennis courts, jacuzzi and a restaurant. €100.

▲ A BRISA DO MAR

Restaurants

A Brisa do Mar

Complexo Balnear do Caniçal, Caniçal ☏ 291 960 726. Daily 10am–midnight. This swish, glass-fronted restaurant by the sea pools serves up superb meat, fish and seafood, such *caldeirão* stew. Expect to pay upwards of €20 a head. For something simpler, there's also an adjoining café.

Miradouro da Portela

Sítio da Portela ☏ 291 966 169. Daily 9am–10pm. A bar-restaurant with two popular wood-panelled front rooms, warmed by log fires on cool evenings. If these are full, there's also a spacious back room with hooks in the ceiling from which hang the house speciality: succulent meat kebabs skewered on long metal poles. The good-value menu also features salads.

Café Piscinas

Porto da Cruz ☏ 917 464 079. Daily 9am–8pm. This little café-restaurant by the seafront pools has a great terrace facing the Atlantic and serves superb sandwiches, salads and fresh sardines from around €6.

Praça da Engenho

Rua da Praia, Porto da Cruz ☏ 291 563 680. Daily 10am–10pm. Cosy, stone-clad restaurant, set back from the seafront and serving decently prepared, moderately priced Madeiran food. There's also a café-bar area with better sea views.

Bars

Beira Mar

Caniçal. Daily 8am–10pm. Right on the seafront, with outdoor tables facing the waves, this friendly café-bar serves drinks, sandwiches and tasty *doses* (snacks) such as octopus, winkles and prawns.

Praia da Lagoa

Praia da Lagoa, Porto da Cruz. Daily 10am–10pm; restaurant 7pm–10pm. Smart, glass-fronted building facing the beach, with a range of sandwiches and snacks. In the evening, the inside area turns into a slightly pricey restaurant serving meat and grilled fish. The area out front hosts occasional summertime discos.

The west

Tourism has yet to make major inroads into the dramatic and unspoilt west coast, and much of the rocky coastline is backed by steep wooded slopes, vineyards and banana plantations and dotted with small villages linked by the coastal highway – only Ribeira Brava and Calheta have anything approaching resort status. West of Calheta, below towering cliffs, nestle Jardim do Mar and neighbouring Paúl do Mar, both burgeoning surf centres. Above here, the wooded valleys offer some superb walking terrain around the village of Prazeres and inland at Rabaçal, perhaps the most beautiful valley on the island. Rabaçal marks the edge of the wild mountain plateau Paúl da Serra, a great destination for walking or a picnic.

Ribeira Brava

Rodoeste bus #7 or #142 (6–9 daily; 50min–1hr 15min). Located at the foot of a dramatic gorge and endowed with an attractive seafront, the buzzing resort of Ribeira Brava makes a good day-trip from the capital, especially in June for the Festa de Saõ Pedro (June 28–29), celebrated with music, dancing and processions.

Ribeira Brava translates as the "angry river", a reference to the river which still comes alive after heavy rains, especially in the autumn, though at other times it's a decidedly meek affair. The town grew up in the fifteenth century as a staging post on the trade routes from the north to Funchal, and its sheltered position also favoured the cultivation of sugar, at that time the island's major crop.

The main focus of the town is the pedestrianized seafront, giving onto a wide, stony beach and lined with a series of bustling cafés and restaurants; there are sunbathing areas and small sea pools to the west of

▼ IGREJA DE SÃO BENTO, RIBEIRA BRAVA

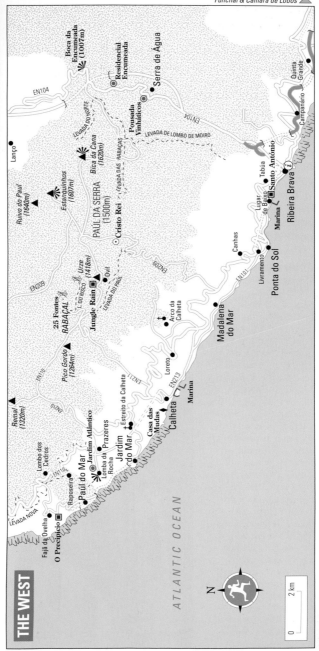

THE WEST

ATLANTIC OCEAN

N

0   2 km

Visting Ribeira Brava

Buses from Funchal come into town on the ER104, close to the main church, while boats from Funchal moor at the jetty to the east of the bay. The **tourist office** (Mon–Fri 9am–12.30pm & 2–5pm, Sat 9.30am–noon; ☎291 951 675) is located on the seafront in a small stone tower, the Forte de São Bento, originally built to protect the town from pirate attack.

the bridge. The town market, decorated with attractive modern azulejos, and the main shopping street, Rua Visconde da Ribeira Brava, are west of the tourist office.

The graceful Igreja de São Bento (daily 7am–1pm & 3–7pm) is a sixteenth-century church with some wonderful Manueline touches, including a stone font and pulpit carved with plants and animals. The characteristic chequered-tiled roof is one of the most beautiful in Madeira.

Ethnographical Museum

Rua de São Francisco 24. Tues–Sun 10am–12.30pm & 2–6pm; €2.50. Ribeira Brava's small Ethnographical Museum is set

PLACES The west

▼ RIBEIRA BRAVA

in a pink sixteenth-century town house, formerly a rum distillery and later a water-powered sugar-cane and cereal mill. Since 1996 it has housed a museum dedicated to local crafts. Although the displays aren't exactly thrilling – fishing boats, mill equipment and looms – they do give an insight into the development of the fishing and weaving trades and the importance of wine and cereals to the area. There's a pleasant café here and some evocative old black-and-white photos of the village.

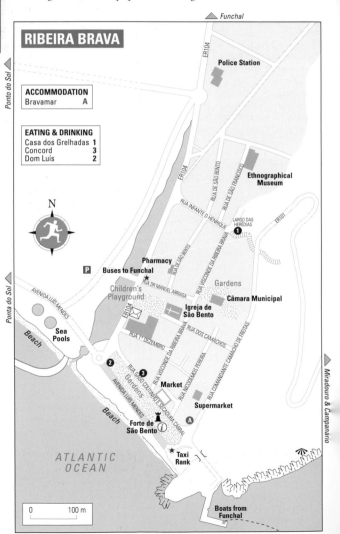

RIBEIRA BRAVA

△ Funchal

Police Station

ACCOMMODATION
Bravamar   A

EATING & DRINKING
Casa dos Grelhadas   1
Concord   3
Dom Luís   2

N

ER104

RUA DE SÃO BENTO

RUA DR FRANCISCO

Ethnographical Museum

RUA INFANTE D HENRIQUE

LARGO DAS HEREDIAS

ER101

RUA DE SÃO BENTO

RUA VISCONDE DA RIBEIRA BRAVA

Pharmacy

P   Buses to Funchal

RUA DR MANUEL ARRIAGA

Children's Playground

Gardens

Câmara Municipal

Igreja de São Bento

RUA 1° DEZEMBRO

RUA VISCONDE DA RIBEIRA BRAVA

RUA DOS CAMACHOS

RUA COMANDANTE CAMACHO DE FREITAS

AVENIDA LUÍS MENDES

Sea Pools

Beach

RUA GAGO COUTINHO E SACADURA CABRAL

AVENIDA LUÍS MENDES

Gardens

Market

RUA NICOLAOMES FERERA

Supermarket

A

Beach

Forte de São Bento   (i)

ATLANTIC OCEAN

★ Taxi Rank

0   100 m

Boats from Funchal

Ponto do Sol ◁

Ponto do Sol ◁

Miradouro & Campanário ▷

Ponta do Sol

A quiet and pretty little village with a relaxed and lively air, Ponta do Sol is reputedly the sunniest spot on the island – its name literally means "sunny point". The population of just 4500 is shoe-horned into the folds of a steep valley, overhung with dense banana plantations; some 600,000 kilos of bananas are shipped from here to Portugal annually.

The town's Baroque church, Nossa Senhora da Luz, on Rua Dr João Augusto Teixeira, was built in the eighteenth century on the site of an older medieval structure and contains some fine seventeenth-century decorative azulejos.

A plaque on a house at nearby Rua Príncipe Dom Luís I marks the birthplace of the grandparents of American novelist John dos Passos (1896–1970), likened to James Joyce and known for his novels *42nd Parallell*, *USA* and *Manhattan Transfer*. The author, who visited the house, is now commemorated in the neighbouring Centro Cultural John de Passos, a modern cultural centre which often has exhibits related to him, along with other events.

Facing a palm-tree-lined seafront, the town beach consists of a stretch of coarse grey stones, though diving platforms are anchored offshore in summer. Head up past the lofty Sol Poente restaurant to the town's jetty, built in the

▲ PONTA DO SOL

nineteenth century, and the only link with the outside world until just after World War II. Head out of town the other way, to the west, for the old road to Madalena do Mar, a great windy stretch through rock tunnels.

Calheta

Rodoeste bus #107 & #142 (1–3 daily; 2hr 30min). Calheta, little more than a village set in a steep valley just above the coast, is growing in popularity thanks to having Madeira's only golden sand beach. Locals say the sand is only borrowed – specially imported from Morocco, most of it ends up getting washed back to Africa after heavy storms – but the beach has attracted a fair amount of development along a seafront

▲ NOSSA SENHORA DA LUZ, PONTA DO SOL

promenade, up to a new yachting marina to the east.

Calheta was given its town charter in 1502 and was governed by Zarco's children. It later became a customs post for sugar exports, but waned in importance with the decline of the sugar trade in the nineteenth century. But sugar cane still fuels the nineteenth-century Engenhos da Calheta (Mon–Fri 8am–6pm, Sat & Sun 9am–6pm; free), a working rum distillery. You can wander round the rather antiquated-looking collection of steam-powered cogs and wheels, used to grind, press and extract the juice from the raw cane (usually April–May). You'll also see the large fermentation vats, where the juice is distilled into *aguardente* white rum. There's usually a chance to taste the rums and *ponchas* or buy some from the souvenir shop.

Just uphill from here, the village church, Igreja Matriz, dates back to 1430, though most of it was rebuilt in 1639. Whilst its exterior is unexceptional, it's worth looking inside if you can (the church is often locked) to see a gloriously ornate ebony and silver tabernacle donated by Manuel I, and the Moorish-inspired Mudejar ceiling.

Casa das Mudas

Vale de Amores. ☎ 291 822 808, Tues–Sun 10am–7pm, major exhibitions €5. Dramatically perched on a clifftop high above Calheta, this cultural centre has become Madeira's leading exhibition space, hosting shows devoted to leading international artists such as Dalí, Picasso and Francis Bacon. The centre is partly set in the sixteenth-century former home of Zarco's granddaughter and partly in a modern extension that seems to merge into the ground – grey interlocking cubes half built into the cliff. The café (Tues–Thurs 10am–6pm, Fri & Sat 10am–10pm) commands spectacular views over the coast. To reach the centre by road, take the turning signed to Estrela from the roundabout at the top of Calheta.

Jardim do Mar

Rodoeste bus #115 (Mon–Fri 1–2 daily; 2hr 45min). Set below a steep, verdant hillside, the traditional

▲ BANANA TREES, JARDIM DO MAR

▲ WALK FROM PRAZERES TO PAÚL DO MAR

fishing village of Jardim do Mar is an instantly likeable place, consisting of a warren of cobbled, traffic-free alleys and laden for much of the year with the scent of honeysuckle. You could easily while away a day or two here strolling along the beach or up into the banana plantations on the slopes above the village. It's also an important surfing centre, hosting an annual championship in January, though backwash since the construction of a sea wall has somewhat spoilt its previously superb surf.

The centre of the village is full of neat wooden street signs and carefully tended paths. From the main square, a road heads east to a little stony beach, which marks the eastern end of a seafront promenade that wends below the village. Follow this and you'll make out the village of Paúl do Mar to the west, set beneath majestic cliffs (see p.142).

To the west of the village, above the church, a neat cobbled path leads past the local shop to a T-junction. You'll see a sign marking a footpath to Paúl do Mar, though the three-

to four-kilometre walk is only possible at low tide. You'll need to arrange transport for your return journey, as the beach is not exposed long enough for a two-way walk. Check locally for tide information.

Next to the sign is a glass case containing a *rede*, a kind of hammock. These were traditionally used as a sort of stretcher for ferrying around the sick or wealthy and would have been carried by two men known as *rodeiros*. In the nineteenth century, this particular *rede* was the favoured mode of transport for a local overweight priest who got his *rodeiros* to carry him as far as Ponto do Pargo, Calheta and even Funchal – the steepness of the cliffs round here makes this seem cruel in the extreme.

Prazeres and the Levada Nova

Rodoeste bus #115 & #107 (1–2 daily; 2hr 45min). Clustered round a twin-spired church, the small agricultural settlement of Prazeres is a good place from which to start walking the nearby Levada Nova, which

A walk from Prazeres to Paúl do Mar

The *Hotel Jardim Atlântico* (see p.146) at Lomba da Rocha, near Prazeres, marks the starting point for a spectacular seventy-minute walk down the cliffs to the seaside village of Paúl do Mar. From the top of the cliff, the boats below look like tiny specks, and there is total silence but for the sound of cicadas and birds. Clearly signed steps to the far side of the hotel car park lead down the pot-holed cliff face. From here the path descends dramatically; after a while you'll see a waterfall behind you, then you cross a stone bridge for the final section. A left-hand turn will take you to the quay of Paúl do Mar (see below). To avoid climbing back up the cliff again it's best to arrange someone to collect you or to order a taxi either from Prazeres or from the restaurant *Largo-Mar* (see p.148) in Paúl do Mar; the ride will cost around €20.

finishes at Ponta do Pargo (see p.149), taking in the village of Raposeira en route – a three- to four-hour walk in all. The Levada Nova is one of the island's most attractive *levadas*, winding through idyllic, largely wooded countryside. For much of the way it shadows the gentle gradients of the coast road 101. The *levada* stops above Ponta do Pargo, and a signed track points you down to the village itself.

Paúl do Mar and around

Rodoeste bus #107 (1–2 daily; 3hr 15 mins). Until an access road was built in the 1960s, Paúl do Mar could only be reached by sea, and though it can now be accessed by a tunnel linking it with neighbouring Jardim do Mar, getting to Paúl do Mar from the Prazeres road is all part of the fun, each loop and turn revealing heady views of the village below. After the exciting approach, the small fishing village is something of an anticlimax, despite its spectacular location beneath towering cliffs. There are some interesting backstreets round the church at its eastern end, while the beach, obscured by a hefty sea wall, occasionally hosts surf competitions.

▼ CHURCH, PAÚL DO MAR

Walks from Rabaçal

A walk from Rabaçal to Risco Waterfall

Follow the steps downhill below the guesthouse for the easy 1km walk to the Risco Waterfall. The steps lead onto the mossy Levada do Risco path. Keep to the upper, right-hand path which follows the *levada* through tranquil woodland – look out for trout in the *levada* waters, specially bred to keep insects at bay. The valley becomes gradually steeper and narrower, and after around twenty minutes you'll reach the sheer sides at the valley's end, with the narrow Risco Waterfall spilling down a high mossy cliff. You can go quite close to the falls along the *levada* wall. The *levada* actually passes right under the waterfall, partly through a tunnel, but this section is gated off and and decidedly dangerous.

A walk from Rabaçal to 25 Fontes

For a more strenuous 2.1km walk – around an hour there and a little longer back – follow signs from the government rest house to 25 Fontes (going left where the path splits to Risco). Go down some steps and turn right onto the Levada das 25 Fontes; for a while it runs parallel to the *levada* to Risco, but at a lower level. Take more steps down and you'll see Risco Waterfall after about fifteen minutes. At the head of the valley, cross a bridge and take the steps uphill. The *levada* is quite narrow for the next fifteen minutes.

You then reach an arched stone bridge where a right-hand turn takes you to 25 Fontes – literally 25 springs, an enchanting jumble of little waterfalls and rivulets – though 25 is probably an exaggeration. This is a lovely spot to have a picnic, assuming there aren't too many other walkers who have got here first.

A walk from Rabaçal to Cristo Rei

Another interesting but very different five-kilometre *levada* walk, the Levada do Paúl, heads off from the car park above Rabaçal. It takes around eighty minutes and ends up at the Cristo Rei, a miniature version of Rio's Christ statue, built in 1962 and also known as Nosso Senhor do Montanha (Our Lord of the Mountain). The walk starts at the small reservoir opposite the car park and heads off in a southeasterly direction – look for a tiny chapel marking the spot where the *levada* comes out of a channel. You pass a couple of streams, but for the most part the landscape consists of lonely moorland, bracken and gorse, with superb views down to the south coast on a clear day. The *levada* crosses the EN209 – the road from Paúl da Serra to Ponta do Sol – a short way downhill from a car park just below the Cristo Rei statue.

You'll have to walk back the way you came unless you want to chance hitching a lift on the little-frequented road.

Rabaçal

No public transport. Among forested mountains high above the coast, Rabaçal is one of the most beautiful valleys on the island. Set in a breathtaking, densely wooded valley, its trees draped in lichens, Rabaçal is completely uninhabited and untouched by the outside world, except for a small government rest house with public toilets and a few stone picnic tables.

Rabaçal is also the starting point for two popular *levada* walks: one to Risco Waterfall (3km from the car park), the other to 25 Fontes (3.7km). Both walks are signed from the rest house, though go early or late in the day to avoid the numerous guided walks which visit from around 10.30am. Just above Rabaçal, a very different walk can be had across rugged moorland to the Cristo Rei, a small statue of Christ. All three walks are described in the box on p.143.

To reach Rabaçal, you can take a shuttle bus (€3 return) from a car park by a gravel *miradouro* viewpoint, or it's a pleasant half-hour walk down a single-track road from the car park.

Paúl da Serra

No public transport. Paúl da Serra, which translates roughly as "mountain plain", is a wild, high plateau which soaks up the winter rain and feeds the *levadas* throughout the year. On clear days it's delightfully empty and fresh, with spectacular views down to the north and south coasts, great for walks or a picnic. When wind or mist sweeps across the boggy ground, however, it can be bleak in the extreme. The plateau is 1300m high and covers an expanse of moorland 17km by 6km, the flattest area on the island and one of the few places where it's safe for cows to wander freely without the risk of falling down a precipice. In summer, when bilberry trees bear fruit, local youngsters often come up to the plateau to camp. Bird-watchers are also attracted by linnets, goldfinches and the rare Berthelot's pipit, found only here and on the Canaries. The sole buildings here are the shepherd's hut and the little hotel and café complex at Urze (see p.148).

Bica da Cana

No public transport. Bica da Cana is the impressive setting for

▼ RABAÇAL, VIEW FROM REST HOUSE

▲ PAÚL DA SERRA

another government rest house. The house is about ten minutes' walk from the main road up a stone track; there's a *miradouro* just above it at a height of 1620m, with fantastic views on clear days. The peak here is actually all that remains of a volcanic cone, from one of Madeira's most recent eruptions – some 890,000 years ago. In summer, this is a very popular picnic spot for Madeirans, especially at weekends.

From Bica da Cana the E204 begins to descend along the edge of a dramatic, craggy mountain valley and you suddenly realize how high up you are as the road pitches through rough road tunnels – keep your windscreen wipers at the ready as mini waterfalls often crash over the car as you enter or leave the tunnels.

Boca da Encumeada

Rodoeste bus #6 and #139 (3–4 daily; 2hr; avoid those that bypass Encumeada via the tunnel, signed "via túnel"). A small layby at the junction of the EN204 and 104 marks the Boca da Encumeada, the "mouth of altitude", a pass at 1007m which marks the highest point of the road linking the north and south coasts. On a clear day you can see the coast at São Vicente in the north and Ribeira Brava in the south; at other times you look down on a surreal sea of white clouds.

Hotels

Báia do Sol

Rua Dr João Augusto Teixeira, Ponta do Sol ☎ 291 970 140, ⊕ www.enotel .com. This controversial modern hotel now takes up most of the village seafront, though at least its facade looks traditional. Inside is a somewhat bland but comfy four-star, complete with small indoor pool, café and sun terrace. The top-floor rooms

▼ BOCA DA ENCUMEADA

(€12 extra) with sea-facing balconies are best. €95

Bravamar

Rua Comandante Camacho de Freitas, Ribeira Brava ☏ 291 952 220, ⓔ hotelbravamar@hotmail.com. Modern seafront three-star hotel at the eastern edge of Ribeira Brava, with its own pool and restaurant. Most rooms have a sea view, and there are also suites and apartments for longer stays. €50, or €60 with sea view.

Calheta Beach

Calheta ☏ 291 820 300, ⓦ www .calheta-beach.com. On the edge of Calheta's sands, this very good-value modern four-star hotel makes a good retreat if you want a quiet spot by the sea. Facilities include a pool, terraces, sauna, gym, satellite TV in all rooms, and a restaurant; staff can also arrange watersports. Good low-season discounts. €50, or €70 with sea view.

Residencial Encumeada

Feiteiras, Serra de Água ☏ 291 951 282, ⓦ www.residencialencumeada .com. A couple of minutes south of the Boca da Encumeada pass, on the EN104, the *Residencial Encumeada* was built in 1999 but has a traditional feel, with tasteful wooden decor. Rooms are large and comfortable, each with a bath, TV and stunning mountain views from their balconies. The spacious downstairs bar-restaurant offers reasonably priced grills and Madeiran staples, while reception has details of great local walks. €40.

Estalagem Casa de Chá

Sítio da Estacada, Prazeres ☏ 291 823 070/1, esolprazeres@mail.telepac.pt. Located just before the church right in the centre of Prazeres, this modern low-rise place is tastefully decorated in traditional style with an attractive garden at the back. All rooms come with satellite TV and a terrace. There's also a pricey restaurant and bar. €55.

Estalagem da Ponta do Sol

Quinta da Rochinha, Ponta do Sol ☏ 291 970 200, ⓦ www.pontadosol .com. Perched on a cliff, five minutes' walk above Ponta do Sol, this sleek hotel was designed by local architect Tiago Oliveira. Rows of white cube-like rooms with balconies and minimalist decor sit on a steep terrace interspersed with lawns. The best rooms face the sea, others the town. There's a small indoor pool and a surreal clifftop outdoor one – its surface flush with its sun terrace – plus a clifftop bar. The glass-fronted restaurant does reasonably priced Madeiran dishes and pasta. €115, or €130 with sea view; discounts for longer stays.

Jardim Atlântico

Lombo da Rocha, Prazeres ☏ 291 820 220, ⓦ www.jardimatlantico .com. For location, this four-star development, five minutes' drive from Prazeres, is hard to beat, stacked on the lip of a 400-metre-high clifftop affording dizzy views over the coast below. The main building contains studios for two people (with their own balconies and kitchenettes), with apartments and bungalows (for two or three people) arranged on terraces below. The complex has its own restaurant, gym, pool, tennis courts, sauna, whirlpools, hydro-massage and a "nudist terrace" (popular with Germans), while spa treatments include "chocotherapy" facials and therapeutic barefoot walks. There's also a games room, live entertainment and even a hotel supermarket, while local walks and bike rental can also be arranged. €110, bungalows from €135.

Jardim do Mar

Sítio da Piedade, Jardim do Mar ☎ 291 823 616, ✉ marnoia@hotmail.com. Right on the main square, this plush hotel has decent-sized rooms offering exhilarating sea views, though the animal heads stuck to the corridor walls are off-putting. There's also a bar and a reasonable restaurant with a superb sea-facing terrace. €76.

Moradia Turistica Cecilia

Jardim do Mar ☎ 291 822 642, ✉ pontajardim@hotmail.com. Its balconies usually draped in drying wetsuits, this characterful guesthouse with its own sea-facing garden is a popular spot with local surfers, and offers simple, clean rooms. It's at the west end of town – follow the signs. €40.

Pousada Vinháticos

Serra de Água ☎ 291 952 344, 🌐 www.pousadadosvinhaticos.com. A great base for walks, Madeira's only *pousada* (historic inn) is set in a stone building with a modern wooden annexe and a few separate log cabins. It has a friendly, Alpine feel with cosy, small rooms, leafy gardens and a highly rated restaurant. There's also a basement bar, a good place to hole up on cool evenings. Best of all are the views of the dramatically rising peaks all around. €70, log cabins from €90.

Cafés and bars

Concord

Rua Gago Coutinho e Secadura Cabral, Ribeira Brava. Daily 6am–11pm.

▲ VIEW FROM POUSADA VINHÁTICOS

One of the best places on the seafront for ice creams, croissants and snacks, served inside or on the attractive esplanade facing the sea, where there are tables under shady trees.

Joe's Bar

Jardim do Mar. Mon–Sat 8.30am– 11pm. A lively café-bar selling fresh fruit juices and snacks at the western end of town by the local shop, with a little beer garden and a few benches outside on the street.

O Precipício

Fajã da Ovelha/Paúl do Mar ☎ 291 872 425. Daily 8am–10pm. Aptly named café-restaurant on the road from Prazeres down to Paúl do Mar – it really does feel as if it's on a precipice, especially when you're on the terrace. Specializes in grills, but also does a good range of drinks and snacks, with a mind-blowing view.

Restaurants

Casa dos Grelhadas

Largo dos Herédias, Riberia Brava ☎ 918 096 654. Tues–Sat 11am–3pm

& 7–11pm, Sun 11am–3pm. Specializes in grills, as its names suggests, with dishes such as *frango no espeto* (chicken kebab) and *alheira da caça* (game sausage). Outdoor tables are set on an attractive raised terrace overlooking a little square. Very good value, with mains from €7.

Dom Luís

Rua Marginal da Vila, Ribeira Brava ☎291 952 543. Daily 8.30am–midnight. This seafront restaurant is a great place for beef, chicken or tuna, all grilled over an open fire. Full meals cost around €15–20.

Jungle Rain

Ovil, Paúl da Serra ☎291 820 150. Daily noon–9.30pm. Part of the *Estalagem Pico da Urze* complex, this is a rather incongruous Disneyesque jungle-themed restaurant filled with mock flora and plastic jungle animals and complete with animal noises and a mini waterfall. If you're here with children it will seem like a godsend – there's even a special kids' menu – while for adults there are grills and pasta dishes from around €9.

Largo-Mar

Paúl do Mar ☎291 872 394. Daily 9am–9pm. At the western end of the beachfront, this is a good place for drinks or meals. Serves fine local fish, including *lapas* (limpets), *caramujos* (winkles), as well as grills at bargain prices; there are outdoor tables, too.

Madelena Mar

Sítio da Vargem, Madelena do Mar ☎291 972 081. Daily 10am–midnight. This excellent little restaurant sits on the main road in the small village halfway between Ponta do Sol and Calheta. Food is varied, generous and

good value, with dishes such as *caldeirão* fish stew and fresh trout for around €10. There's also a small garden area and parking.

Rocha Mar

Sítio da Vila Calheta ☎291 823 600. Tues–Sun noon–midnight. Opposite Calheta's marina, with a few outdoor tables and a moderately priced menu of tasty fresh fish and grills.

Santo António

Lugar de Baixo ☎291 972 868. Daily noon–midnight. Modern seafront restaurant with its own terrace facing the waves and very good-quality food at reasonable prices – though these may increase when the neighbouring marina is fully operational. It's just outside the tunnel on the road leaving Ribeira Brava towards Ponta do Sol.

Sol Poente

Cais do Ponta do Sol, Ponta do Sol ☎291 973 579. Tues–Sun noon–11pm. Perched on top of a dramatic rocky outcrop overlooking the water, the *Sol Poente* café is a great spot for a drink or a snack, especially at sunset. For a full meal, head to the restaurant over the road, partly built into the side of the cliff, but with good views from the upstairs windows and superbly cooked dishes including *lapas* (limpets) brought sizzling to your table. Mains from €7–9.

Tar Mar

Sítio do Piedade, Jardim do Mar ☎291 823 207. Daily noon–midnight. Above the cobbled lane to the beach with seating indoors and out, this restaurant offers tasty fresh grilled fish and seafood along with fine specials such as *arroz de lapas* (limpets and rice) and salads for around €12–15.

Porto Moniz and northwestern Madeira

A trip to the northwest of the island is a must if you want to see Madeira's beauty at its rawest and most dramatic – even if the weather tends to be less clement. With its little lighthouse atop sheer cliffs, Ponta do Pargo marks the westernmost edge of Madeira. In the far northwest, Porto Moniz's natural sea pools and spectacular position make it the prime spot in the north, while nearby is the alluring walk along the Levada da Central. Heading east, the coast road hugs the dramatic contours of the mountains that spill down to the sea, connecting the picturesque village of Seixal with São Vicente, one of the prettiest on the island, home to a series of extraordinary underground caves and a volcano museum.

Ponta do Pargo

Rodoeste bus #142 (1–3 daily; 3hr 30mins). The small village of Ponta do Pargo, "Sea bream Point", was so named because Zarco caught sea bream here while exploring the area. The village is surrounded by fields of vines and vegetables, worked on by hardy-looking women wrapped in headscarves and carrying huge bundles on their heads. At the village centre is an attractive church whose terrace overlooks fields and the lighthouse below, spectacularly sited atop sheer cliffs at the westernmost point on the island.

You can walk to the lighthouse (signed "Farol") from the church

▲ LIGHTHOUSE, PONTA DO PARGO

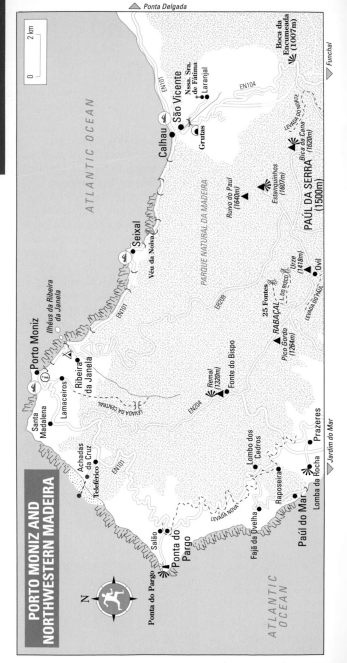

PORTO MONIZ AND NORTHWESTERN MADEIRA

N

0   2 km

Ponta Delgada

Funchal

Boca da Encumeada (1007m)

Nssa. Sra. de Fátima
Laranjal
EN104

EN101

São Vicente
Calhau

Grutas

ATLANTIC OCEAN

LEVADA DO NORTE
Bica da Cana (1620m)

PAÚL DA SERRA (1500m)

Ruivo do Paul (1640m)
Estanquinhos (1660m)

PARQUE NATURAL DA MADEIRA

Seixal

Véu da Noiva

EN101

Urze (1418m)
L DO BISPO
Ovil
LEVADA DO PAÚL
25 Fontes
RABAÇAL
Pico Gordo (1264m)

Ilhéus da Ribeira da Janela

Porto Moniz

ER208

Remal (1320m)
Fonte do Bispo

EN204

Santa Madalena
Lamaceiros
Ribeira da Janela
LEVADA DA CENTRAL

Achadas da Cruz
Teleférico

EN101

Lombo dos Cedros

Prazeres

Jardim do Mar

Raposeira

LEVADA NOVA

Lomba da Rocha

Paúl do Mar

Fajã da Ovelha

Salão

Ponta do Pargo

Ponta do Pargo

ATLANTIC OCEAN

in about twenty minutes: follow the signpost to Salão de Baixo downhill past a farm and through low, twisted vines, and when the path joins a bigger road, turn right. If you're driving, follow signs for "Farol".

Just north of the Ponta do Pargo you can join the Levada Nova, which runs east to Prazeres – see p.141 for details of the walk in the other direction.

Achadas da Cruz Teleférico

Mon–Fri 8–9am & 11am–8pm, Sat & Sun 7.30–8am & 11am–8pm; closes 6pm from Oct–March. €3 return.

From Ponta do Pargo the EN101 cuts through remote countryside to the little village of Achadas da Cruz, worth a detour for its *teleférico* (cable car), built to help farmers tend their fields on the local *fajã* – the flat, fertile soil at the bottom of a cliff, formed originally by landslides. The single car plummets down on a scarily-thin cable – you can also walk

▲ FONTANARIA, SÃO PEDRO, PONTA DO PARGO

the 4.5km to the bottom and take the cable car back (allow a good two hours).

Porto Moniz

Despite being as far away from Funchal as it's possible to get, Porto Moniz is the north coast's liveliest and most developed town, with a cluster of cafés,

▲ PICNIC SPOT, PONTA DO PARGO

PLACES

Porto Moniz and northwestern Madeira

PORTO MONIZ

EATING & DRINKING
Cachalote 1
Gaivota 4
Mar Vista 2
Salgueiro 3

ACCOMMODATION
Calhau A
Euro Moniz B
Youth Hostel C

ATLANTIC OCEAN

Ilhéu Mole

Sea Pools

Aquarium

Taxi rank

Sea Pools

SÍTO DAS POÇAS

Centro De Ciência Viva

Harbour

Seixal

Buses to Funchal

Pharmacy

Police Station

THE OLD TOWN

Taxi rank

ESTRADA REGIONAL EN 101

Câmara Municipal

0   100 m

▽ Lamaceiros & Achadas da Cruz

restaurants and hotels gathered round its main attraction, two sets of natural sea pools, at either end of a seafront promenade.

The town was originally named Ponta do Tristão, after the nearby headland, which marked the dividing point between the two captaincies – the administrative areas run by Zarco and Tristão Vaz Teixeira during the early colonial days. From 1533, the town was run by Francisco Moniz – who later married Zarco's granddaughter – and in 1577 it was renamed after him. Protected from the elements by the offshore islet,

Ilhéu Mole – Porto Moniz became a major whaling centre when Azorean whalers set up here in 1939, but until tourism began to make an impact in the late twentieth century, few outsiders visited, its residents relying on whaling and the produce of the steep agricultural terraces. On the slopes around the old town you'll still see fields lined with heather broom fences, which shelter vines and crops from the northerly winds.

Porto Moniz sea pools

Porto Moniz's new town extends between the natural sea pools

Visiting Porto Moniz

Rodoeste **buses** #80 and #139 (1–3 daily; 3hr 30min–4hr) from Funchal pull up close to the harbour. There's a small but helpful **tourist office** (Mon–Fri 10.30am–4.30pm; ☏291 850 193) close to the western sea pools. There is usually no short-age of places to park, unless you visit during the town's main festival, **Semana do Mar** (29 June–6 July), a week of sea-related festivities and events.

▲ SEA POOLS, PORTO MONIZ

that have formed in the sculpted volcanic rocks. The easterly pools, below the *Restaurante Cachalote* (see p.159), consist of a series of interconnecting channels and shallow plunge pools, which get deliciously warm in summer, though sunbathing space on the surrounding rocks is usually at a premium.

The pleasant seafront promenade, lined with kiosk cafés, continues west for 500m or so to the second set of more formal sea pools, most of which have been augmented with concrete. Entrance costs €1.

Porto Moniz Aquarium

Daily 10am–6pm; €7. Imaginatively built below a mock stone fort, the town's aquarium showpieces species native to Madeiran waters, with tanks set into artificial rocks and cave-like rooms. Sadly the collection of fish and crustacea is extremely limited and barely worth the entrance fee; the café on the roof may prove more appealing.

Centro de Ciência Viva

Tues–Sun 10am–7pm. Temporary exhibitions around €5. Just back

from the seafront promenade, the glass-fronted Centro de Ciência Viva (Centre for Living Science) hosts science-related temporary exhibits. Primarily aimed at locals, so not always with English labelling, the exhibits can be first-rate, some having moved on from London's Science Museum. It also has a cybercafé and shop.

▼ PORTO MONIZ

The road from Porto Moniz to São Vicente

The 16km of the old EN101 road from Porto Moniz to São Vicente is one of the most expensive stretches of road ever built. The original road was started in the early twentieth century and was completed by hand at a rate of about 1km a year – it took sixteen years in all. The road and tunnels had to be hacked out of sheer slopes and cliffs; at times workers had to be suspended by ropes to dig out the steeper sections. By the end of the twentieth century, the increased volume of traffic had turned the narrower sections of the thoroughfare into dangerous bottlenecks, so new tunnels have been cut along these sections, boosting the cost of the road, but making the route much less harrowing.

Porto Moniz old town

While the seafront continues to sprout new hotels, the old town, stacked up on the hill behind, remains largely unaffected by tourism. Here you'll find a couple of banks with ATMs and a mini-market for groceries.

If you have your own transport, zigzag up the hillside behind the village, where the views become more and more dramatic, with a couple

▼ WATERFALL ON ROAD TO SÃO VICENTE

of *miradouros* to pull in at. Continue up this road for the start of one of the island's loveliest walks, along the Levada da Central (see below).

The Levada da Central da Ribeira da Janela

This walk (2hr 20min round-trip, or can be shortened to 1hr 20min) takes you up a dramatic valley into UNESCO-protected lauraceous forest, some of the oldest surviving woodland in Europe. To get to the start point, drive or take a taxi the 3km from Porto Moniz to Lamaceiros. Go through the village past the church, then head straight on down a track where the road doubles back on itself. You'll see a small reservoir on your left: you can park here and walk down to the reservoir, to the right of which is the start of the *levada*.

The *levada* is easy to follow, with handy picnic tables set out at regular intervals, and takes you past rows of agapanthus and

▲ VIEW FROM SEIXAL

hydrangeas, dazzling in summer. After five to ten minutes, you'll see the Ribeira da Janela river way below you in the valley on the left.

A few hundred metres further on, the path crosses a filtration plant. All along this stretch you'll see swifts swooping below you in the valley and hear scurrying lizards. After fifteen minutes from the start, you dive under the shade of dense trees until you emerge again to find a picnic table with stunning views down to the sea and the village of Ribeira da Janela across the valley.

After twenty-five minutes, you pass another picnic table, not long after which the *levada* briefly disappears under the path. Just beyond where it re-emerges you reach a sluice; walk along the side of the sluice – not up the path to the right – for more great views. The next section of 200m is lined with fruit trees, shortly beyond which is another picnic spot.

After forty minutes from the start, you'll see the top of the valley, a mass of dense green foliage – this is the lauraceous woodland. From here, the path narrows in sections, with gradually steeper drops. You can either turn back here, or continue for another thirty minutes, climbing the valley until the path ends where the *levada* disappears into a tunnel.

Seixal

Rodoeste bus #139 (1–3 daily; 3hr 15 min). Seixal is a quiet little town on the dramatic north coast. The through road passes the functional upper town, where you can find shops and cafés. As you enter the upper town from the west, a signed track heads down to the Piscinas Naturais (natural sea pools), a smaller version of those at Porto Moniz.

Further east, follow the signs for the *cais* (quay) to reach the prettier lower town, a tranquil cluster of traditional houses, connected by steep cobbled steps and interspersed with vineyards, all set against a backdrop of towering mountains. Look out for the Véu da Noiva (bride's veil) waterfalls pouring down the cliff and over a road tunnel further down the coast.

The quay itself is usually full of bobbing fishing boats. You can take the steps down to the sea for some great swimming, or, when the waves get up, you can swim in the small sea pools just behind the quay.

São Vicente

Rodoeste bus #6 (3–4 daily) and #139 (1–3 daily); 2hr 30min. Sitting at the junction between the north-coast highway and the pass over to Funchal, São Vicente has always been a popular stopping-off point for Madeirans travelling from the north coast to the capital – and, more recently, its spruced-up old town has become similarly popular with tourists. The central zone is completely pedestrianized and

ridiculously pretty, its narrow streets lined with flowers and neatly kept cafés and shops, all gathered round a lovely seventeenth-century Baroque church with a chequered spire. Inside, there's a painting of São Vicente – Lisbon's patron saint – on the ceiling and beautiful azulejos on the lower walls. In front of the church is a cobbled square, surrounded by palm trees and with a carefully tended cemetery to one side.

From the town you can also see the distinctive church tower of Nossa Senhora de Fátima, completed in 1953, on the hilltop opposite, splendid in its solitude against a backdrop of green mountains.

Calhau

A kilometre north of São Vicente, Calhau comprises an appealing row of restaurants and shops facing a rocky beach. Though popular with surfers, the Atlantic here is usually far too dangerous to risk swimming, and copious amounts of driftwood get deposited on the stones – the wood is often burned in giant pyres on the beach. While at the seafront, take a look at the unusual Capela São Roque, by the bridge – a rock pile with a cross on it and a chapel embedded in its front, dating from 1692.

Heading east over the bridge, it's a couple of minutes' walk along the seafront to the Piscina

▼ SÃO VICENTE

▲ NOSSA SENHORA DE FÁTIMA

Calamar (open daily; free), a lido in front of the *Estalagem Calamar*. There are seawater pools and ladders down to the sea – though you should avoid swimming when it's rough.

Grutas e Centro do Vulcanismo

Daily 10am–7pm, last entry 6pm; tours every 15–20min; 1hr. €8. The Grutas de São Vicente is a dramatic series of underground caves, with the added attraction of an informative exhibition on volcanoes at the adjoining Centro do Vulcanismo. The well-signed entrance has a car park (reached by an underpass), and the small café and exhibition space will help you to fill in time while you wait for the next tour.

The caves were blasted out by volcanic gases during Madeira's last eruption some 890,000 years ago; the longest cave is about 1km long and they descend some 40m underground at their deepest point. Water slowly filters through the porous rock to form a series of clear, cold rock pools and streams – you

may feel it dripping on your head. The caves have been lit and considerably modified since the Brit James Johnson stumbled upon them in 1855 – now you can walk upright comfortably through most of the cave tunnels, their chocolate-coloured roofs rippled like mousse.

The tour ends at the Centro do Vulcanismo which has exhibits about volcanoes round the world, and an interesting video on Madeira's volcanic past. You can be transported in a shaking "lift" to the "centre of the earth", a rather tame hall of mirrors showing a replica earth's core, and don 3D glasses to view a very average film showing a volcanic eruption.

Hotels

Residencial Calhau

Sítio das Poças, Porto Moniz ☎291 853 104, ⓦwww.residencialcalhau.web.pt. This imaginatively designed and friendly place has decent, bright rooms with private bathrooms and small balconies overlooking the sea pools. There's a sunny breakfast room and an upstairs games room with satellite TV and sweeping views. Good value. €40.

Estalagem Brisa Mar

Seixal ☎ 291 854 476, ☏ 291 854 477. Decent, if simple, rooms with private bathrooms above a restaurant on the harbourfront. There are great sea views from the front rooms, though not all have balconies. €40.

Estalagem do Mar

Juncos-Fajã da Areia, Calhau ☎ 291 840 010, ⊛ estalagemdomar.com. Just west of the bridge on the seafront, this unattractive but well-equipped low-rise modern block has decently sized – and decently priced – rooms. All come with bath and TV and have either sea-facing balconies or open onto a lawns near the hotel's outdoor pool, which is surrounded by neatly landscaped gardens. Other facilities include an indoor pool, sauna, gym, jacuzzi, tennis courts and an in-house restaurant serving expensive traditional Madeiran dishes and seafood. €60.

Estalagem Praia Mar

Calhau ☎ 291 840 100, ☏ 291 842 749. This prominent, traditional-style building with green shutters sits at the west end of the row of restaurants facing the sea. All the rooms are large and airy, though the higher ones at the front – some with balconies – have the best views. Also has its own, good-value restaurant. €40.

Euro Moniz

Porto Moniz ☎ 291 850 050, ⊛ www .euromoniz.com. A modern high-rise with mostly sea-facing rooms, each with contemporary decor, balconies and cable TV. There's also a small indoor pool, a sauna and gym and a panoramic bar. Good value. €50, or €55 for sea views.

Youth Hostel

Vila do Porto Moniz ☎ 291 853 915, ⊛ www.pousadasjuventude.pt. The titchy hostel in the old town has just one double room and three dorms of 4–8 beds, so phone ahead, especially as it is not always staffed. Dorms, some with sweeping views, are fine and there's also a kitchen and common room. €6 per person or €20 a double.

Campsites

Parque do Campismo

Ribeira da Janela ☎ 291 853 872. Set on a series of flat grassy terraces in a narrow river valley, just below the hamlet of Ribeira da Janela, this fairly new campsite is set in rural solitude. Decent facilities and good nearby walks, but you'll need a car to get here.

Cafés

Estoril

Largo de Igreja, São Vicente. Daily 8am–8pm. Right opposite São Vicente's historic church, with outdoor tables on the pedestrianized square, this is the perfect spot to enjoy pastries, inexpensive snacks or drinks.

O Farol

Salão de Baixo, Ponta do Pargo. Daily 10am–9.30pm. This modern café-restaurant is built in traditional stone, a little uphill from the lighthouse. Along with sandwiches and soups, it does a range of well-prepared grills and salads from around €10.

Gaivota

Porto Moniz. Daily 8am–midnight.
An all-purpose affair (bakers,
pastelaria, café, pizzeria and
restaurant), with a back terrace
facing the sea and a good menu
that features moderately priced
pizzas, octopus and grilled
chicken.

Restaurants

Brisa Mar

Seixal ☎291 854 476. Daily 8am–
10pm. This smart establishment
is the best place to eat in
Seixal, with a large dining area,
snappy service and views over
the harbour; the fresh fish is
the thing to go for, though the
salads and omelettes are equally
good.

Cachalote

Porto Moniz. ☎291 853 180. Daily
noon–4pm. Porto Moniz's
largest restaurant, open for
lunch only, attractively built
on the rocks right next to
the eastern sea pools. There's
even a mock tunnel inside
connecting two of the dining
rooms, one of which has
space for 600 diners – it only
gets remotely full when tour
coaches pass by. The cuisine
includes good-value fish
bouillabaisse, lobster and the
usual Madeiran dishes.

Ferro Velho

Rua da Fonte Velha, São Vicente.
☎291 842 763. Daily 8am–2am.
The menu of fish and meat
dishes is somewhat limited,
but this place wins thanks
to its location in the heart
of the historic centre and its
shady outdoor patio. Inside,
the pub-like decor includes
international soccer scarves,
from Ajax to Man Utd.

Mar Vista

Porto Moniz ☎291 852 949. Daily
11am–10pm. Friendly and
popular with locals, offering a
good range of fish, meats, salads
and soups from around €9. It
also has an attractive sea-facing
terrace.

Salgueiro

Porto Moniz ☎291 852 139. Daily
10am–midnight. The best dining
spot in Porto Moniz, with a
raised, sea-facing terrace, swift
service and decent soups, tasty
garlic bread and a range of full
meals from around €10.

O Virgílio

Calhau ☎291 842 467. Daily
10am–10pm. This place tends
to attract more locals than the
neighbouring restaurants on
this stretch on the seafront
thanks to its inexpensive grilled
meats and fish, which are
served inside or on the veranda.
There's also an attractive,
azulejos-lined bar.

Bars and clubs

O Corvo

Rua da Fonte Velha, São Vicente.
Daily 8am–1am. Any modicum
of nightlife to be had in São
Vicente can be found here, a
small pub with an old still in
one corner and bank notes
pinned to one wall. There are
low stools inside and a TV
often showing live sport,
with a couple of outdoor
tables.

Kalhau's

Cais do Seixal, Seixal. Sun–Thurs
9am–2am, Fri & Sat 9am–4am.
Surprisinly hip decor and varied
sounds for such a remote place,
with billiards and table football
to boot.

PLACES Porto Moniz and northwestern Madeira

Northern Madeira

Densely forested mountains rise up dramatically from Madeira's spectacular north coast. Much of the woodland is made up of lauraceous forest, so ancient it has been designated a **UNESCO World Heritage site.** Tiny Ponta Delgada is the only place on the coast, though the superb road via **Boaventura** to **Arco de São Jorge** rewards you with a dazzling rose garden. **Santana** is famed for its triangular-shaped houses, and also boasts a fine theme park and a hair-raising cable-car ride. It's also the gateway to the island's best inland walking country, around **Queimadas,** and its highest peak at **Pico Ruivo,** which can also be reached on the superb peak-to-peak trek from **Pico Arieiro.** Equally impressive is the towering rock known as **Penha de Águia,** which casts a shadow over the pretty mountain village of **Faial.**

Ponta Delgada

Rodoeste bus #6 (3 daily; around 3hr). The quiet, traditional fishing village of Ponta Delgada is overlooked by walls of forested mountains. Its main attraction is a modern lido complex (signed "Piscina"), the social hub of the village in summer. Here you'll find a deliciously fresh sea pool (€1), changing rooms and a fine café-restaurant. A couple of hundred metres west, the Igreja do Bom Jesus takes

▼ SEA POOLS, PONTA DELGADA

centre stage for the
September Festa de
Senhor Jesus, a religious
festival commemorating
the survival of a
wooden crucifix,
washed ashore in 1470,
presumably from a
sinking ship. A chapel
was built to house
the crucifix, but this
burnt down in 1908.
The crucifix, however,
"miraculously" survived
the fire and, though
charred, takes pride of
place in the current
church, constructed in
1919.

▲ BOAVENTURA

Boaventura

Rodoeste bus #6 (3
daily; 3hr 15min). Set in verdant
countryside, Boaventura is a
small, agricultural hillside village
clustered round a church with a
cobbled terrace. Just below the
church, a sign points you to a
miradouro, from where there are
magnificent views of the coast
and the towering mountains to
the north. Continue down this
road for a few kilometres to
another small lido complex by
the sea.

From Boaventura, the old
road to Arco de São Jorge
is one of the most dramatic
in Madeira, twisting up the
verdant, precipitous valley of
the Ribeira do Pôrco before
plunging through a tunnel and
winding back down to the coast
through more lush farmland and
vineyards.

Arco de São Jorge and the Rosarium

Rodoeste bus #6 (3 daily; 3hr 45min)
or São Gonçalo bus #103 (2–4
daily; 3hr). Gardens daily: May–Sept
11am–7pm; Oct–April 11am–6pm.
€5. Set against a green wall of

trees rising up the neighbouring
mountains, Arco de São Jorge
is little more than a tiny village,
but boasts one of the most
attractive self-catering villa
complexes on the island, the
Quinta do Arco (see p.173) and
an impressive *roseiral* (rosarium).
With its entrance at the lovely
old Quinta do Arco manor
house, signed just off the main
road, the rosarium is the largest
collection of roses in Portugal.
Come in summer when most
of the thousand species are in
bloom and the gardens are truly
spectacular. Some of the rare
and unusual species include
climbing China roses, tea and
damask roses and modern
hybrids.

São Jorge

São Gonçalo bus #103 (2–4 daily;
around 2hr 40min). The spruce
little village of São Jorge (Saint
George) is made up of well-
kept houses set among vineyards
and radiating out from an
eighteenth-century Baroque
church. The highly elaborate

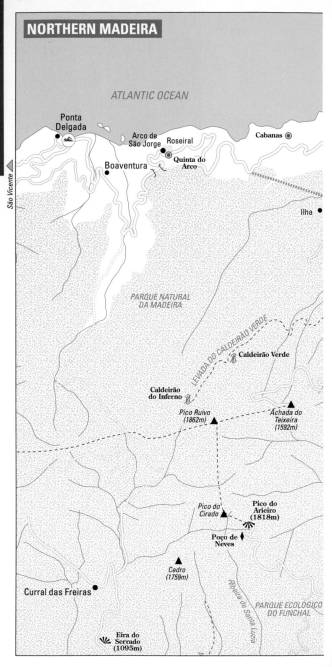

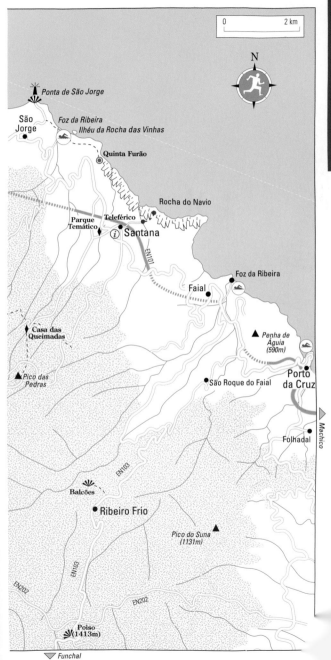

▲ ALTAR, SÃO JORGE

gold-leafed altar contains a statue of Saint George slaying the dragon and there are also some lovely azulejos. Behind the church, the Casa de Palha (literally "house of straw") is a traditional thatch-roofed building that has been maintained as a little souvenir shop and café (daily noon–8pm), though the food isn't up to much.

You can see other *casas de palha* on the pleasant fifteen-minute walk north of São Jorge to its little red-topped

lighthouse on the Ponta de São Jorge.

A kilometre or so beyond São Jorge, a sign points left to **Foz da Ribeira**, consisting of sea pools by a small stony beach. It's a lovely drive there, via a narrow road running parallel to the Ribeira de São Jorge past vineyards and neat terraces. The road ends by a stone footbridge over the river – the halfway point of the coastal walk from São Jorge to Quinta Furão (see box opposite). Here you'll

The coastal walk from São Jorge to Quinta Furão

São Jorge's church marks the starting point of an exhilarating two-hour coastal walk to *Quinta Furão* (see below), via the pool at Foz da Ribeira. From the church, head towards the sea and take the first right at the small chapel. After around five minutes the road ends at a cemetery. Take the cobbled steps to the left and cross a narrow road; you'll pick up the path slightly to the right. From here it's a steep, winding, twenty-minute descent to the ruins of Calhau, an old port. Turn right onto the coastal path and after five minutes you'll come to the old bridge and lido at Foz de Ribeira, a great spot to cool off with a swim (see opposite). Continue over the bridge and you'll see the path in front of you, zigzagging up the hill. Just over an hour from the bridge, the path rejoins civilization near the neat lawns of the *Quinta Furão* (see below), where you can stop for a drink. From here it's a further 4km by road to Santana; you could get the quinta to order a taxi or alternatively walk to the main road and catch bus #103 (2–4 daily) to Santana or back to São Jorge.

find the Complexo Balnear de São Jorge, a modern sea pool complex, open year-round, with its own café-restaurant and superb views up the coast.

Quinta Furão

Dramatically sited on clifftops and surrounded by vineyards, the *Quinta Furão* is a hotel and restaurant complex (see p.173) run by the Madeiran Wine Company. During the September harvest (usually the second or third week of the month) tourists are encouraged to join in the traditional grape-treading – bare footed, with men stripped to the waist. It's all totally geared up for tourists, but free and fun nevertheless. At other times, you can visit the highly rated restaurant. It also marks the start or finish of the walk to or from São Jorge via Foz da Ribeira (see box above).

Santana

Santana, named after St Anne, is famed for its distinctive A-frame houses, something of a symbol of Madeira (see box on p.167). You'll see several of these dotted round the surrounding farmland – the richly fertile soil supports

vines along with various fruits, including figs, mulberries, plums and kiwi fruits. The village itself is fairly ordinary, clustered round some neatly tended squares and a pretty church, though its proximity to some of Madeira's most impressive mountain scenery makes it a handy base for a night or two. If your visit coincides with the February Festa dos Compadres or July's

▼ SANTANA

Visiting Santana

Santana can be reached by São Gonçalo bus #56 (1–4 daily; 1hr 40min) or #103 (2–4 daily; 1hr 40min). The **tourist office** (Mon–Fri 9.30am–1pm & 2.30–5.30pm, Sat 9.30am–noon; ☎291 572 992) is just off the main through road next to the town hall inside a traditional Santana house – there are a couple of others that you can visit next door. Below the town church you'll find a supermarket, while opposite and just uphill there are a couple of banks, shops and local cafés.

folk festival (see p.200), you'll see the place at its liveliest.

The Rocha do Navio Teleférico

Wed & Sat 9–10am, noon–12.30pm & 6–7pm (5–6pm from Oct–April). €3.50 return. Below Santana's church, a signed road leads about 1km downhill through farmland to the Rocha do Navio Teleférico, a small cable car which plummets terrifyingly down a sheer cliff to Rocha do Navio, a cultivated *fajã* on a rocky foreshore. The service, though popular with tourists, is geared towards farmers working on the *fajã*, hence the odd operating times. As you descend, there are fine views of the coast and of a gushing waterfall spilling down sheer rock walls. When the weather's calm you can swim off the stony beach at the bottom.

Parque Temático do Madeira

Daily: April–August 10am–7pm; Sept–March 10am–6pm. €10, children under 14 €8, under 5s free. Set in seven hectares of landscaped grounds on a steep slope, the Parque Temático do Madeira (Madeira Theme Park) is a fun half-day out if you have children. The main attractions consist of various low, concrete pavilions offering multimedia shows on aspects of Madeira and island life: its people, environment, future and so on. The shows are a bit hit or miss and you'll probably want to

have good breaks between each one or the novelty soon palls. Luckily there's plenty of space for children to run around, with a boating lake, rides, cafés and shops as further diversions. There's also a playground, a toy train, a re-created water mill, models of Madeiran houses and historical forms of transport. The most interesting part, for adults at least, is the *artesanato*, a craft village with demonstrations of traditional crafts such as carving and weaving.

Queimadas

Inland from Santana lies one of Madeira's most enchanting and least-spoilt forest areas (part of the UNESCO-protected lauraceous forest). *Queimadas* means "burning" – traditionally people brought combustible goods to burn here, safe in the knowledge that the cool, damp air would prevent fires from getting out of control.

To get there follow the sign to Queimadas off the main EN101 just before the Parque Temático. An incredibly steep road leads to the Casa das Queimadas, an idyllic-looking thatched government rest house, used by forestry workers and overhung with dazzling red-flowered camellia trees. The inside of the place is pretty basic, but you can use its toilets if needed. In front of the house there are wooden picnic tables under tall trees draped with angel hair moss and lichens, next to bubbling streams, where geese roost in mini Santana houses – a great spot for a picnic or an afternoon chilling out, as many locals do at weekends.

Many people also come up here to walk the Levada do Caldeirão Verde (see below), one of the best *levada* walks on the island. If you fancy a shorter walk (30min each way), look for the sign by the end of the road which directs you onto a gentle wooded path to Pico das Pedras, a picnic spot on the road linking Santana with Achada do Teixeira and Pico Ruivo (see p.168).

The Levada do Caldeirão Verde

The three- to four-hour (13km) return walk along the Levada do Caldeirão Verde takes you through laurel woods and across some extremely steep terrain. Good footwear, waterproofs and a torch are essential and a jumper can be useful, as the air at this height is cool and most of the walk is in shade. Rainfall is also common.

The start of the *levada* is clearly signed from the Casa das Queimadas. Follow the path under ancient pine trees until you reach a gate, which you go through. Five minutes beyond here, a steep arrowed detour takes you down to the right round an unstable section of wall, but it quickly climbs to rejoin the main *levada* path.

The path narrows and you have to walk on the *levada* wall as it follows the twisting contours of the valley. After twenty minutes or so, you get superb views of the densely wooded mountains. Look behind and you can see right down to the north coast.

After about an hour from the start, the *levada* passes through four tunnels which get progressively longer and lower. In the third tunnel, keep to the side of the path to avoid deep puddles. In the fourth tunnel watch your head, too, as the roof is low in sections.

For the last half an hour, you'll be walking on a *levada* wall that is just 40cm wide with fairly steep drops. At one stage you pass a huge stump of a lily-of-the-valley tree thought to be over eight hundred years old. Finally, after around ninety minutes into the walk, you'll

PLACES Northern Madeira

Santana houses

Known in Portuguese as *palheiros*, or haylofts, Santana houses are tiny thatched houses. Consisting of little more than a ground-floor room with a platform wedged into the roof eaves – like an "A" in cross-section – they are unique to Madeira. Their low, squat shape is ideally suited to withstand the Atlantic weather that often lashes the north coast, the thatched roofs reaching down almost to the ground to protect the interior from the rain. The upper rooms form sleeping quarters, while the downstairs area is traditionally used for storage or as a living area. People cooked outside to avoid the risk of fires, and toilets were also well clear of the living area.

The houses first appeared in the early seventeenth century, but lost favour during the last century as modern building techniques – and Madeiran living standards – improved. A few Santana houses are still inhabited – mainly thanks to government incentives to attract tourists – but the majority of them now house cattle, with corrugated iron roofs replacing the expensive thatch.

reach a green amphitheatre of moss-covered rock, the Caldeirão Verde. A small path leads to the bottom of a waterfall trickling into a small lake, a pleasant spot for a picnic. The *levada* path continues, partly up steps, to Caldeirão do Inferno (Cauldron of Hell), an even more impressive waterfall about an hour further on, but it's a tough, tricky stretch, and unless you're an experienced walker it's best to turn back at Caldeirão Verde.

Pico Ruivo and around

At 1862m, Pico Ruivo (Redhead Peak) is Madeira's highest point, offering the most breathtaking views over the island. Despite its height, the peak is a relatively short walk from the narrow EN101-5 road (clearly signposted off the main EN101 coast road) from Santana to Achada do Teixeira. Around 10km from Santana, the road passes **Pico das Pedras**, an attractive wooded picnic spot and a good base for some local walks. The road then climbs onto the barer lower slopes of Pico Ruivo until it ends some 15km beyond Pico das Pedras at a car park next to the somewhat ungainly **Achada do Teixeira** government rest house. Behind the house is an impressive series of natural basalt columns known as **Homem em Pé**, the "standing man". The grassy surrounds make a good place for a picnic and on a clear day you can see right down to the north coast from here.

Back at the car park, you will see the start of a paved path to the summit of Pico Ruivo, a relatively easy 2.2km walk along a flat ridge; allow around an hour and a half to two hours return. After forty minutes you'll see Pico Ruivo's government rest house, a small white building. Just before here a path heads off steeply to the left; this leads on to Pico do Arieiro (see p.170), while the other way a path is signed to the Encumeada pass (11km; see p.145).

Northern Madeira   **PLACES**

HOMEM EM PÉ

From the government rest house, it's a steep but short climb to a series of viewing platforms at the summit. It's a wonderful spot: wisps of cloud and smoke-like mist drift below you or creep up from the valleys, and there is complete silence apart from the sound of the wind and the odd hardy bird. To the southwest, the valley sides tumble down to the tiny red rooftops of Curral das Freiras (see p.110), while to the west spin the distant wind turbines on Pául da Serra, almost at the same height. Southeast lie the huge craggy peaks of Pico das Torres and Pico Arieiro.

▲ PENHA DA ÁGUIA FROM FAIAL

Penha de Águia, Faial and around

SAM bus #53 and #78 (1–5 daily; 1hr 25min). It's easy to see how Penha de Águia ("Eagle Rock") got its name. A sheer-sided rocky cube rises to 590m, its lower half terraced into fields, the upper half a craggy wilderness where ospreys nest. A small road skirts the lower slopes of the rock and there are extremely tough footpaths up to its summit – about an hour and a half's climb, and only suitable for the very fit.

Otherwise, the best place to contemplate the rock is from the quiet hillside village of Faial, which takes its name from an evergreen shrub, the wax myrtle (*faia* in Portuguese), that grows in the area. The best views are from its cobbled square, centred on a substantial oak tree. The nearby church is the focal point of an annual *romaria*, a lively village festival held on September 8.

From Faial, a road bridge crosses the deep valley of the Ribeira Sêca. You can head under the new bridge to Foz da Ribeira do Faial, past a karting track to a little lido complex. A sea pool, kids' playground, rocky beach and a seasonal café attract a lively crowd in summer.

Ribeiro Frio

São Gonçalo bus #56, #103 or #138 (1–2 daily; 1hr). Roughly halfway between the north and south coasts is the tiny village of Ribeiro Frio, "cold river" – named because of its high and secluded position in a wooded valley which gets little sun. But the cool air doesn't stop the flora from thriving: pride of Madeira, hydrangeas and orchids give colour to the well-tended village gardens by the river. The village's main sight, however, is a government-run trout farm, set in attractive gardens with giant tree ferns and impressive topiary. Fed by several local *levadas*, the circular freshwater tanks are a teeming mass of swirling fish, from tiny spry to large trout, some of which end up on the menus of local restaurants.

The woodland around Ribeiro Frio is part of the lauraceous forest native to Madeira and forms the backdrop to some great walks, the most popular being the gentle twenty- to thirty-minute return walk to **Balcões**. Signed off the bottom end of the village, just after Bar Faisca, it's an easy walk, past luxuriant gardens and along a flat woodland path. Balcões is a wooden viewing platform, which offers sweeping views over the island's highest peaks. A tougher walk from Ribeiro Frio is signposted off to the east to Portela (see p.131), a twelve-kilometre hike taking three to four hours.

▼ RIBEIRO FRIO TROUT FARM

Pico do Arieiro

Although only the third-highest point on Madeira at 1818m – so high that the mountain top is often well above the cloud line – Pico do Arieiro's accessibility makes it the most popular of the peaks and attracts a steady stream of visitors. Get there very early or late in the afternoon to avoid the biggest crowds.

As the road climbs up the increasingly barren slopes, a small sign to the left points out the Poço de Neves (snow well), an igloo-shaped hut built in 1800. Before electric refrigeration, ice was stored here before being carried down to local hospitals; the ice was also used to supply gin and tonics at *Reid's Palace Hotel*.

From the summit car park, the views can be astounding, with both coasts of the island sometimes visible, though, more often than not, at least one of the coasts will be submerged beneath fluffy clouds, itself an impressive sight. If you're unlucky, the summit will be shrouded in cold mist.

The car park marks the start of one of the most rewarding walks on the island, across to Pico Ruivo (see below). Another option is to walk just the first section of the route to Pico Ruivo, as far as Ninho da Manta (the Buzzard's Nest), clearly signposted off the main path. This is a relatively easy fifty-minute round-trip walk to a dizzy *miradouro* with fantastic views down to the south coast. Remember, however, that the return walk is uphill.

Walk from Pico do Arieiro to Pico Ruivo

This walk (5.6km or 7km each way depending on the route

▲ CRAFT STALL NEAR BALCÕES

taken) is the most spectacular on Madeira – and consequently one of the most popular. Unless you've arranged for someone to meet you at Achada do Teixeira, at the other end see below, you'll need to allow around five to six hours for the tough round trip. Alternatively, consider taking one of the numerous organized walks (see p.197), which include pick-ups at Achada do Teixeira. It's best to set off early to get the best views and be free of crowds. Although there are some pretty scary drops at times, the walk is easily manageable if you take sensible precautions, wear good boots and take a torch.

The clearly signed path heads off from Pico do Arieiro's car park along a narrow spine of rock with drops to either side, though any steep parts are fenced off. The first stretch of this walk takes in some startling volcanic landscape, with basalt columns and sills rising like bones through the soft, reddish ferrous soil.

After around 20 minutes you pass the Ninho da Manta viewpoint and descend some steps before passing through a short tunnel under Pico do Gato. An hour into the walk, the path splits. The shorter left-hand route (5.6km total) passes through a series of tunnels, currently closed for repair but due to reopen in late 2008. Until this route is reopened, you'll have to take the tougher right-hand path (7km total), with very steep steps ascending for around an hour to the peak of Torre where there are dazzling views towards Pico Ruivo. You then descend steps for another thirty minutes, after which you'll see the other path joining through a tunnel on your left.

The path winds past ancient, 200-year-old heather trees and you'll also see some caves, which shepherds use for shelter. You then climb quite steeply; here the contorted, bleached white branches of the heather trees are intertwined along the edge of the path to stabilize the soil against rock falls.

Two and a half hours into the walk, you come to the Pico Ruivo government rest house, a lovely spot with trees all around (and a public toilet), where most tour groups rest for lunch. The summit of Pico Ruivo is a tantalizing climb above: the path is steep, but it only takes fifteen minutes to reach a series of viewing platforms at the summit (see p.168).

At 1862m, this point has even more spectacular views than Pico do Arieiro (which you can see in the distance). From the summit, either return the way you came to Pico Arieiro (remembering it is more uphill on the return) or, if you have transport to collect you, head back down to the government rest house, from where the path continues for around 45 minutes northeast across a relatively flat ridge to Achada do Teixeira (see p.168).

Poiso and the Parque Ecológico do Funchal

São Gonçalo bus #103 or #138 (1 daily; 30min). The EN103 begins its descent to Funchal at Poiso, a 1400-metre-high mountain pass. Poiso means "resting place", as this was the traditional spot for travellers to stop when going from coast to coast. Many drivers still pause at the excellent *Casa de Abrigo* (see p.174).

The steep slopes to the west of Poiso form part of the Parque Ecológico do Funchal, a protected area used as an outdoor "education centre" for students. You'll see tracks into the park signed off the main Poiso–Funchal road. Inside the park, there are further marked paths, picnic tables and barbecue spots. Its steep slopes, fed by deep bedded water courses, create microclimates that are ideal for a variety of flora and bird life. A practised eye can spot indigenous Til trees, giant species of laurel

▲ PICO DO ARIEIRO, POÇO DE NEVES

such as Loureiro, Vinhático and Barbusano, and birds such as the Manx shearwater, sparrowhawks, red-legged partridges, barn owls, Madeiran robins, blackcaps and firecrests.

Hotels

Cabanas

Sítio da Beira da Quinta (São Jorge) ☎291 576 291, ⓦwww.cabanasvillage .com. Two kilometres west of São Jorge, this tourist complex consists of 25 circular bungalows, each of which sleeps up to two adults and a child. Some of them lie close to the clifftop, with great views (€5 extra) down the coast, though most of them are set back amid lawns. There's a mid-price restaurant, a tiny swimming pool, a craft shop and a bar, along with two re-created Santana houses next to the restaurant. The location is certainly impressive, but the huts – said to have been inspired by Zulu huts after the founder's stay in Africa – are too closely packed together and gimmicky for a stay of more than one night. €70.

Casa de Capelinha

Terreiro, Ponta Delgada ☎291 860 040, ⓦwww.casadacapelinha .com. Stylish designer hotel with white, sea-facing cubist rooms, neat modern decor and grounds which include a small pool, games room and a little restaurant-bar. €57, not including breakfast.

O Colmo

Sítio do Serrado, Santana ☎291 570 290, ⓦwww.hotelcolmo.com. On the main road just up from the post office, this modern four-star hotel is built in traditional style, with decent-sized rooms, all with satellite TV. There's a big restaurant downstairs which often fills up with tour groups. The heated indoor pool, gym and sauna make it all good value. €70.

Monte Mar Palace

Sítio do Montado, Ponta Delgada ☎291 860 030, ⓦwww.montemar-palace .com. A large, ungainly block, but wonderfully sited on a bluff just west of Ponta Delgada. Rooms are comfy, if functional, and come with balconies, air conditioning and large bathrooms. There's a so-so in-house restaurant, indoor and outdoor pools, spa, gym and even a little putting green. Popular with package groups. €50, or €55 with sea view.

Quinta do Arco

Arco de São Jorge ☎291 570 270, ⓦwww.quintadoarco.com. If you want to get away from it all, this complex of cottages sleeping up to four people is a perfect rural escape. Built in traditional style, with wooden stairs and rustic drapes, the cottages each have a living room and kitchenette, with a cosy upstairs bedroom. The grounds are gorgeous, with lush vegetation, an honesty bar and a small pool. €96.

Quinta Furão

Achada do Gramacho (Santana) ☎291 570 100, ⓦwww.quintadofurao .com. This large, modern three-storey hotel is spectacularly positioned in one of Madeira's largest vineyards (see p.165) on a clifftop some 4km west of Santana. The third-floor rooms have balconies with great views over the cliffs. There's also a heated pool and gym, and a restaurant, bar and shop in a separate building 50m down the hill (see p.175). €120.

Solar de Boaventura

Serrão Boaventura, Boaventura ℡291 860 888, ⓦwww.solar-boaventura.com. Very plush and imaginatively designed hotel set amidst a huge expanse of lawn in a valley just off the road to Santana. The original *solar* (manor house) dates from 1776 and served as a school and medical centre before its current reincarnation as the hotel reception and pricey but excellent restaurant. The *solar* has a series of lavish modern extensions, comprising atriums, plush bedrooms and communal areas. €60.

Restaurants

Casa de Abrigo

Poiso ℡291 782 269. Daily 8am–midnight. A popular mountain café–restaurant, usually smelling deliciously of wood smoke from its roaring fire. Moderately priced specialities include succulent roasted meats, including rich *cozido* stews, though many people get no further than having a *poncha* or two at the bar.

A Chave

Sítio da Igreja, Faial ℡291 573 262. Daily 10am–midnight. Situated opposite the church, this place does sizzlingly good fish and meat dishes at decent prices, and has a lovely terrace garden complete with bird-of-paradise flowers, a small fish pond and distant sea views.

Complexo Balnear de São Jorge

Foz da Ribeira, 1km east of São Jorge ℡291 576 734. Daily 9am–2am. The little restaurant overlooking the sea pools at this lido serves excellent-value, generous

GRUTAS DO FAIAL

portions of fish and dishes such as *arroz de marisco* (seafood rice) and *cozido* (stew) from around €5–6.

Grutas do Faial

Sítio da Degolada, Faial ☎291 572 817. Daily 9am–10pm. Atmospheric café-restaurant with a dining room nestled into a stone grotto and well-prepared meat and fish dishes from €9. It's right by the junction of the main Machico road and the Ribeiro Frio turning (ER103).

Quinta Furão

Achada do Gramacho, 4km west of Santana ☎291 570 100. Daily noon–3.30pm & 7–9.30pm. Reservations are advised for a meal at this fine place, just below the hotel of the same name (see p.173), 4km west of Santana. The slightly formal restaurant offers expensive but unusual dishes from around €14, such as steak *a caldeirão verde* (with pastry and roquefort) and desserts such as ice cream with wild fruits. Vegetarian dishes include grilled vegetables with Santana cheese, and there's an extensive wine list – not to mention a superb view over the cliffs from the front terrace.

Victor's

Ribeiro Frio ☎291 575 898. Daily 9am–6pm. Cosy, wood-lined café-restaurant with a log fire; the reasonably priced menu features local trout, grilled meats, pasta and salads, as well as moderately priced drinks and snacks.

▲ COMPLEXO BALNEAR DE SÃO JORGE

Café-bars

1958

São Jorge. Mon–Fri 7am–1pm & 2–10pm, Sat 7am–1pm. Right by the church, this supermarket-cum-café-bar sees most of the villagers at some point in the day, who pop in for supplies and a swift coffee or drink at the great little stand-up counter.

Piscina

Ponta Delgada. Mon–Thurs & Sun 10am–7pm, Fri & Sat 10am–9pm. Stylish bar-restaurant with groovy coloured plastic seats facing the sea pools. The bar offers cheap beer with *tremoços*, pickled lupin seeds.

Porto Santo

The small island of Porto Santo, just 11km long and 6km wide, lies around 75km northeast of Madeira. It's relatively flat and arid, with a long swathe of pristine sandy beach which attracts droves of summer visitors from Madeira, but it's little visited at other times and remains one of Europe's least discovered beach destinations. Most of the island's five thousand inhabitants live in and around Vila Baleira, the attractive capital where Cristopher Columbus lived for a while. Porto Santo also claims one of the best golf courses in Portugal.

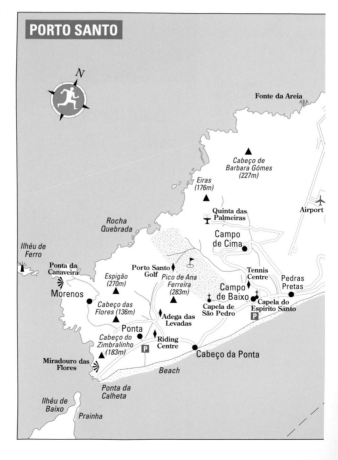

PORTO SANTO

Fonte da Areia

Cabeço de Barbara Gómes (227m)

Eiras (176m)

Quinta das Palmeiras

Airport

Rocha Quebrada

Campo de Cima

Ilhéu de Ferro

Ponta da Canaveira

Porto Santo Golf

Pico de Ana Ferreira (283m)

Tennis Centre

Pedras Pretas

Espigão (270m)

Campo de Baixo

Morenos

Cabeço das Flores (136m)

Capela de São Pedro

Capela do Espírito Santo

Adega das Levadas

Ponta

Cabeço do Zimbralinho (183m)

Riding Centre

Cabeço da Ponta

Miradouro das Flores

Beach

Ponta da Calheta

Ilhéu de Baixo

Prainha

Visiting Porto Santo

See p.191 for details of **ferries** to and from the island and details of public transport. Porto Santo's **tourist office** is in Vila Baleira on Avenida Henrique Vieira de Castro 5 (May–Sept Mon–Fri 8.30am–7pm, Sat 8.30am–1.30pm; Oct–April Mon–Fri 9.30am–12.30pm & 2–5.30pm, Sat 10am–12.30pm, ☎291 982 361), just off the main square. There are **banks** with ATMs at the bottom end of Avenida Henrique Vieira de Castro 5.

Vila Baleira

With its largely sixteenth- and seventeenth-century architecture, red terracotta roofs, cobbled streets and exotic plants, Vila Baleira is as picturesque and lively a village as any on Madeira. The leafy and pedestrianized Avenida Infante Dom Henrique lures you down to its pristine blue flag beach. The town stretch is inevitably

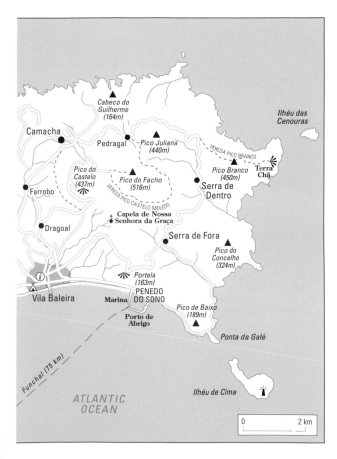

▲ MADEIRA FROM SEA ON PORTO SANTO FERRY

the busiest on the island, but the crowds are rarely overwhelming. The soft sand on Porto Santo is said to have healing properties, ideal for those suffering from eczema, varicose veins or an excess of city living, and elderly folk can often be seen lying buried up to their necks.

Lined with benches, the town jetty is a popular spot for evening walks and young lovers. Just by the entrance to the jetty is the town's little market building and a statue of a Barqueiro, a traditional boatman.

It's a short walk to the palm-shaded main square, the attractive Largo do Pelourinho, containing the village's squat, two-tiered Câmara Municipal (town hall), flanked by sentry-like dragon trees. Adjacent is the white seventeenth-century Igreja de Nossa Senhora da Piedade, built on the site of Vila Baleira's original church, destroyed by pirates in 1667. A decorative azulejos panel adorns the exterior, and there are further azulejos inside.

Casa Museu Cristóvão Colombo

Rua Cristóvão Colombo 12, Vila Baleira. Tues–Sat 10am–12.30 &

A brief history of Porto Santo

Geologically far older than Madeira, Porto Santo was discovered by the Portuguese explorers Zarco and Teixeira in 1418. They docked in its sheltered waters before setting off to explore the more forbidding-looking island of Madeira in the distance. Portuguese colonizers – mainly farmers and fishermen from southern Portugal – settled on Porto Santo from 1420. They planted vines and sugar cane and exploited the native dragon trees for their sap, which could be made into dye. The island's first governor was Bartolomeu Perestrelo, of Genoese ancestry, a friend of Christopher Columbus, who frequently visited the island in the late 1470s.

Unlike its sister island, Porto Santo never really prospered. The dragon trees were quickly felled and crops were decimated by imported rabbits, and between the fifteenth and the eighteenth centuries, Moorish, French and English pirates looted the low-lying, broad coastline more or less at will.

The opening of the airport, partly as a NATO base, in 1960, was a major boost to the economy, and today the island is increasingly dependent on tourism – which is just as well, as drought and deforestation have all but destroyed the island's agriculture.

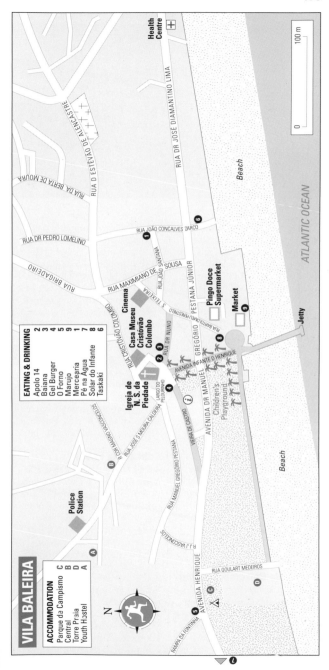

VILA BALEIRA

ACCOMMODATION

Parque da Campismo	C
Central	B
Torre Praia	D
Youth Hostel	A

EATING & DRINKING

Apolo 14	2
Baiana	3
Gel Burger	4
O Forno	5
Marujo	9
Mercearia	1
Pé na Água	7
Solar do Infante	8
Taskaki	6

Health Centre

Police Station

Igreja de N.S. da Piedade

Casa Museu Cristóvão Colombo

Cinema

Children's Playground

Pingo Doce Supermarket

Market

Jetty

ATLANTIC OCEAN

Beach

Beach

RUA D ESTÊVÃO DE ALENCASTRE

RUA DA BERTA DE MOURA

RUA DR PEDRO LOMELINO

RUA BRIGADEIRO

RUA DR DR VASCONCELOS

R DR MARIANO VASCONCELOS

RUA JOSÉ S. MOURA CALDEIRA

RUA CRISTÓVÃO COLOMBO

RUA MAXIMIANO DE SOUSA

RUA JOÃO SANTANA

S TEIXEIRA

RUA DR JOSÉ DIAMANTINO LIMA

RUA JOÃO GONCALVES ZARCO

RUA DR NUNO

RUA PESTANA JÚNIOR

RUA BARTOLOMEU PERESTRELO

GREGÓRIO

AVENIDA INFANTE D HENRIQUE

AVENIDA DR MANUEL

VIEIRA DE CASTRO

LARGO DO PELOURINHO

RUA MANUEL GREGÓRIO PESTANA

R J J VASCONCELOS

AVENIDA HENRIQUE

RAMPA DA FONTINHA

RUA GOULART MEDEIROS

N

0   100 m

▲ JETTY, VILA BALEIRA

2–5.30pm (July–Sept until 7pm), Sun 10am–1pm. €1.50. The island's most famous building, the Casa Museu Cristóvão Colombo was once the home of Christopher Columbus (see box on p.182). Now heavily restored, it comprises an attractive series of rooms displaying artefacts either connected with Columbus or related to the history of the island. There are various portraits of the great man and scenes from his adventures, together with maps of his journeys and models of the boats he sailed in. The downstairs room contains two sunken grain stores, while upstairs lie treasures retrieved from the *Slot ter Hooge*, a Dutch boat owned by the East India Company which sank off the north coast of Porto Santo in 1724 en route to Jakarta. The ship went down with most of its crew, boxes of silver ingots, Spanish and Dutch coins and valuable ceramics.

Campo de Baixo and around

Buses #4 & #7 from Vila Baleira (7–10 daily). Around 4km west of Vila Baleira lies the village of Campo de Baixo. Its small eighteenth-century church, Capela do Espírito Santo, was built when the village was an important farming community – Campo de Baixo means "lower field". Today the sprawling village relies on growing number of shops, cafés and hotels that have grown up a short walk from the superb wide stretch of soft sandy beach. On the beach approach, a small fair ground sets up in summer compete with dodgems and food stalls.

A dirt track just west of the **Porto Santo Tennis Academy** (see p.198) heads up to a viewpoint on the wind-eroded slopes of Pico de Ana Ferreira (283m), a conical volcanic peak.

Cabeço da Ponta

Bus #4 & #7 from Vila Baleira (7–10 daily). Cabeço da Ponta consists of a small cluster of apartments, restaurants and two large hotels just back from the island's widest, most exhilarating part of the beach – though you need to stroll through one of the hotels to access the sands. It makes a great spot for a beach holiday away from it all, the only nightlife consisting of the giant moths that flutter round the hotel lights. The three kilometres between here and Campo de Baixa will become substantially more lively with the imminent opening of two major tourist complexes.

Ponta da Calheta

Bus #4 from Vila Baleira via Campo de Baixo and Cabeço da Ponta (2–4 daily). West of Cabeço da Ponta, the beach, backed by steep dunes, gets quieter and more rugged. At Ponta da Calheta, the sand gives way to volcanic rock sculpted by the elements into wonderfully shaped arches and blowholes. The only building in Ponta da Calheta is the *O Calhetas* restaurant (see p.186), a great spot to watch the sun set on the horizon beside the distant outline of Madeira.

Northwestern Porto Santo

Just off the main road, past Porto Santo's Centro Hípico (see p.199), a left turn takes you to **Miradouro das Flores**, a viewpoint right above Ponta da Calheta offering the island's most spectacular views: you can see right along the length of the beach to one side and over to Madeira on the other. The dusty viewpoint is marked by a statue of deaf Portuguese painter Francisco Maya, a twentieth-century eccentric who loved to paint Porto Santo and asked to be buried at sea between this point and the offshore islet of Ilhéu de Ferro.

The dirt road continues north to **Morenos**, a lovely hilltop picnic spot neatly laid out with wooden tables, barbecue grills and fresh-water taps. Apart from weekends in summer, when locals descend in droves, the hilltop is usually deserted.

Porto Santo Golf

Sítio da Lapeira, ☎291 983 778, ⓦwww.portosantogolf.com. The brainchild of Spanish golfing star Severiano Ballesteros, the Porto Santo golf course is both larger and more challenging than the courses on Madeira. Its greens and fairways stand out in vivid contrast to the arid landscape around it, and the design is heavily influenced by the desert-like environs. The clubhouse is a modern medley of stone, glass and bamboo punctuated with neatly potted cacti. The course itself bends round water features and is all cambers and slopes. There are two nine-hole circuits at present, with plans for another 18-hole course.

Quinta das Palmeiras

Sítio dos Linhaires, ☎291 983 625. Daily: May–Sept 9am–7pm; Oct–April 10am–1pm & 3–5pm. €2.50. Plonked in the middle of one of the most barren parts of the island, Quinta das Palmeiras is a little oasis of greenery, a privately run mini-botanical garden consisting of fruit

▼ STATUE, VILA BALEIRA

Christopher Columbus

Christopher Columbus's links with Porto Santo began in 1478 when he visited the island while working for a Genoese sugar merchant based in Lisbon. He may have been visiting fellow Genoese Bartolomeu Perestrelo, Porto Santo's first governor, or exploring the possibilities of exporting sap from the island's dragon trees. He was soon to return, for in 1479 he married Filipa Moniz, Bartolomeu Perestrelo's daughter, whom he met after a church service in Machico in Madeira. It is thought that they lived on Porto Santo until 1484, in the house which is now Vila Baleira's Columbus Museum. In 1484, they moved to Funchal, where not long afterwards Filipa died giving birth to their son.

During his time on Porto Santo, it is said that Columbus was inspired to set off for America after seeing seeds and wood washed up on Porto Santo's beach, making him wonder if there were land further west. He asked the court in Lisbon to sponsor his explorations, but was refused any help. In 1485, Spain agreed to back his journey, and in 1492 he set off from Palos, landing on the American continent three months later, though at the time he was convinced he had discovered a western sea route to India.

The island celebrates the explorer with an annual **Christopher Columbus Week** in late September. The five-day festival consists of re-enactments of Columbus's landing on Porto Santo in a replica boat, a mock wedding ceremony of the kind that Columbus and Filipa Moniz would have gone through, period musical performances, flag ceremonies and a medieval market.

trees, vines and exotic plants. Imaginatively landscaped paths run past cages of peacocks, love birds, toucans, parrots and finches to a duck pond complete with swans, just below a café. There's even an impressively large rhea. Buses don't call here, but island tours visit, or you could catch a taxi.

Camacha and Fonte da Areia

Bus #1 from Vila Baleira (2–3 daily). The main settlement in the north, Camacha consists of a sprawl of white houses set on a barren slope overlooking the rocky coast. The only local sight is Fonte da Areia, the "spring of the sands", once Camacha's main water supply. The water is said to have healing powers, and for a time it was bottled and sold to Madeira and mainland Portugal, but the process became uneconomic. A series of stone huts and palm trees have grown up round the spring, a tranquil

spot for a picnic. A marked trail winds steeply down a cliff to a wave-battered sandy beach – a pleasant, if tiring, thirty-minute return walk.

Pico do Castelo and Pedragal

The picturesque wooded peak of Pico do Castelo, at 437m the fourth highest on Porto Santo, towers over the island. Reached by a rough, cobbled track, a cacti-lined *miradouro* offers great views of the airport and both north and south coasts. A rusting cannon is the only one that remains of the twelve that once circled the mountain, part of the seventeenth-century fortifications installed by the Spanish during their occupation of Portugal from 1581 to 1640.

From the *miradouro* a path climbs to the summit of the mountain (take the upper track where it splits) and

then continues all
the way to Pedragal,
an abandoned farm,
on the main north-
coast road. However,
if you fancy walking
the entire route
– it takes around
two hours – it's best
to do it in reverse
to avoid ending
your walk in the
middle of nowhere.

▲ THE WALK TO TERRA CHÃ

You could easily get a taxi to
Pedragal, for example, and
after your walk take a bus or
taxi from Camacha back to
your hotel. From Pedragal
the walk to Pico do Castelo
is clearly signposted, though
it's a tough climb, circling the
cedar-topped peaks of Pico da
Gandaia and Pico do Facho en
route. From Pico do Castelo,
however, it's a relatively easy
descent to Camacha.

Terra Chã and Pico Branco

A couple of kilometres east
of Pedragal lies the start of a
signed mountain walk to the
lookout point of Terra Chã
via Pico Branco. It's a four-
kilometre return trek and takes
two to three hours. Perhaps

the best walk on the island, it's
relatively easy and takes in a
diverse landscape, from desert-
like scrub to woodland, with
excellent views all the way. The
path takes you up the steep,
barren slopes of Pico Branco
– if you're lucky you may spot
the rare giant snails that live
here. As you approach the top of
the 450-metre-high mountain
the scenery becomes greener
and wooded. From here the
path continues to Terra Chã, the
northeastern tip of the island,
from where there are superb
views of Ilhéu das Cenouras to
the east.

Serra de Dentro

Bus #2 from Vila Baleira (Mon–Fri
3–4 daily). The deep Serra de

▲ PICO DO CASTELO

Dentro valley was once prime agricultural land, but over the years drought has destroyed the area's prosperity and reduced the tiny village of Serra de Dentro to a ghostly cluster of eerily decaying houses and farm buildings amidst row upon row of deserted, terraced slopes. The valley, however, is a good place to spot rare birds, including kestrels, falcons and crested hoopoes.

Portela

Three kilometres south of Serra de Dentro the road swings round to the *miradouro* at Portela, a superb viewpoint, looking over the beach and harbour below, backed by a row of old traditional windmills.

Beyond here, on a breezy ridge, you'll see the hilltop Capela de Nossa Senhora da Graça, parts of which date back to the fifteenth century, making it one of the oldest churches on the island.

Hotels

Pensão Areia Dourada

Sítio do Espírito Santo, Campo do Baixo ☎ 291 980 110, ⓦ www .paraisodourada.pt. A three-storeyed modern guesthouse on the main south-coast highway, some five minutes' walk from the beach. The good-sized rooms are spotless and come with balconies and private bathrooms. The complex includes a dull restaurant downstairs, offering moderately priced Madeiran staples, a decent café and a shop selling touristy handicrafts and wine. €80, or €85 with sea view.

Residencial Central

Rua C. Magno Vasconcelos, Vila Baleira ☎ 291 982 226, ⓕ 291 983 460. This modern, white, low-rise *residencial* on a hill five minutes' walk from the centre offers the best-value budget option in town. Rooms are spotless and include en-suite bathrooms and TVs and there are sweeping sea views from the upper rooms and

▲ SERRA DE DENTRO

the small, leafy terrace. Facilities include a bar and large breakfast room. €65.

Luamar Aparthotel

Cabeço da Ponta ☏291 984 121, ⓦwww .torrepraia.pt. This low-rise hotel, set on a wide, sandy beach, is ideal for families and self-caterers. Though slightly showing their age, the compact, well-designed apartments (which sleep up to four people) come with living room, bathroom and kitchenette. It's worth paying extra to have an apartment facing the sea rather than the main road, and all rooms come with balconies or – for those on the ground floor – terraces opening up onto lawns. There's a large outdoor pool, a lunchtime café, mini-market, sauna, gym and a daytime courtesy bus to Vila Baleira. Good low-season reductions. €162, or €192 with sea view.

Hotel Porto Santo

Ribeiro Cochino, Campo do Baixo ☏291 980 140, ⓦwww .hotelportosanto.com. The island's most sophisticated hotel, this discreet, low-rise four-star is set in its own palm-studded lawns just back from the beach, with antiques adding a formal air. The modestly sized rooms all have cable TV, air conditioning and balconies facing the lawns or fields at the side. There's a restaurant and terrace facing the outdoor pool with a separate children's

▲ TRADITIONAL WINDMILL, PORTELA

pool. Other facilities include crazy golf, tennis courts and playground; staff can also arrange watersports, horse riding and bike rental. €186.

Hotel Torre Praia

Rua Goulart Madeiros, Vila Baleira ☏291 980 450, ⓦwww.torrepraia .pt. A large, modern four-star hotel right on the beach in the west of town, imaginatively constructed round the stone tower (*torre*) of an old cement factory which dominates the reception area. The best rooms are those on the upper floors with sea views; lower ones overlook lawns to the side. There's a small pool, restaurant, squash court, gym, sauna, jacuzzi and direct access to the beach. The panoramic bar (daily from 9pm) offers fine views. €220.

Hotel Vila Baleira

Sítio do Cabeço da Ponta ☏291 980 800, ⓦwww.vilabaleira.com. Located in Cabeço da Ponta, this pink high-rise hotel has 256 rooms and a separate annexe with 56 apartments. Both blocks are set back from the sea on the wrong side of the coastal highway and bizarrely skewed so that none of the large, functional rooms directly face the Atlantic. Nevertheless, the international-standard facilities are first-rate, with an in-house restaurant, indoor pool, shops, games room, children's room and bar. A tunnel under the road leads to a highly rated thelassotherapy centre (open to non-residents), along with an open-air pool, children's play area and a restaurant for barbecued sardines, chicken and pizzas. The hotel also lays on live entertainment. €175.

Youth Hostel

Sítio das Matas, Vila Baleira ☏291 982 607, ⓦwww.pousadasjuventude .pt. Porto Santo's modern youth hostel is located at the top end of Vila Baleira, with good views over the island. Divided into male and female blocks, there are 11 dorms of three beds and eight of four, plus one double bedroom (€20). Dorm beds €8.

Campsites

Parque de Campismo Porto Santo

Rua Goulart Madeiros, Vila Baleira ☏291 983 111. Porto Santo's only campsite occupies a spacious sandy enclosure just off the highway. The basic facilities include a children's play area, cold showers and limited shade in the form of a few trees and bushes.

Cafés

Gel Burger

Largo do Pelourinho, Vila Baleira. Daily 8am–2am. The liveliest café in town, with outside tables sprawling out onto the main square beneath palm trees and everything from morning coffee and croissants to light meals, pastries, cakes, ice creams and drinks. The counter usually has a fine range of meat and tuna rissoles.

Marujo

Praça do Barqueiro, Vila Baleira. Daily 8am–2am. Adjacent to the main market, this modern, wood-panelled café-bar has boppy sounds and a great terrace facing the jetty; outside tables nestle under palm trees.

Restaurants

Baiana

Rua do Dr Nuno S. Teixeira 7, Vila Baleira ☏291 984 649. Daily 11am–4pm & 6.30–2am. The best place in town for a full meal, this airy, wood-ceilinged restaurant just east of the main square is always busy. There are superb starters such as cheeses, olives and garlic bread. Main courses are around €12 and include barbecued chicken, grilled prawns, *bife na pedra* (steak cooked on a stone) and *caldeirada* (stew). Fresh fish usually includes *bodião* (parrot fish), *badejo* (coal fish) and octopus. Leave room for the tasty desserts and milkshakes.

O Calhetas

Calheta ☏291 984 380. Daily 10am–10pm. With a smart, minimalist interior, this bar-restaurant offers the best – and priciest – beachside food on the island, while the outdoor terrace offers great views of Ilhéu de Baixo and distant Madeira. There are a few meat dishes, though the place is best known for its fresh fish and seafood such as *caldeirada* (fish casserole), seafood *açorda* (with bread sauce) and giant spicy prawns. Full meals run to about €25 a head, or just visit the attached bar for drinks, ice creams and snacks such as octopus sandwiches. Phone ahead and the restaurant will pick you up from your hotel and drive you back again afterwards.

Estrela do Norte

Sítio da Camacha, Camacha ☎ 291 983 500. Daily 10am–4pm & 7pm–2am. People from all over the island visit this highly rated *churrascaria* for its superior, if slightly pricey, grilled meat and fish served in a modern, barn-like, stone-clad room with wooden benches. There are also a few outdoor seats on a gravel forecourt or under a covered porch.

O Forno

Rampa da Fontinha, Vila Baleira ☎ 291 985 141. Daily 11am–11pm. Bustling, good-value place with a modern decor of wood and chrome tables and chairs, offering traditional barbecue-grilled *espetada*, and meats, along with home-baked bread. Plain and simply grilled chicken is often the best bet at around €9. The entrance is opposite the campsite on the main south coast road.

Mar e Sol

Estrada do Forno da Cal, Campo de Baixo ☎ 291 982 269. Daily 10am–midnight; closed Tues Sept–May. A traditional-style restaurant with an outdoor terrace on a raised bit of dune, overlooking a wide swathe of beach. Moderately priced specialities include tuna steaks, *fragateira* (fish stew) and other fish dishes from around €11. The speciality is *feijoada* (bean stew) for two for €30.

Pé na Água

Rua das Pedras Pretos, Pedras Pretos ☎ 291 983 114. Daily 11am–11pm. Just out of Vila Baleira, the "foot in the water" is an arty restaurant which blends modern design with a rustic beach look. Food and service are first rate, with moderately priced pasta and fish from €11 and more pricy seafood, including *arroz de marisco* or *cataplana* for two for €30. There are outside seats on decking facing the beach.

Solar do Infante

Praça do Barqueiro, Vila Baleira ☎ 291 985 270. Daily noon–midnight. Right by the jetty, this swish, stone-clad restaurant has a sleek glass-and-steel interior. Service is slick but dishes such as "harmony of salmon and shrimps" and seafood spaghetti start at a reasonable €12 or so.

Bars

Apolo 14

Rua do Dr Nuno S. Teixeira 3–5, Vila Baleira. Daily 8am–2am. Locals prop up the bar in this small bar-restaurant on the main square, with Coral beer on tap and walls lined with crusty bottles of wine. Families also pop in for coffee, ice creams or inexpensive meals served at a couple of indoor tables or out on the square. It also serves Vinho do Porto Santo, the sherry-like local wine.

João do Cabeço

Sítio do Cabeço, Cabeço da Ponta. Daily 1–4pm & 6pm–1am. On the

▲ CHALLENGER BEACH BAR, PENEDO SONO

main road between the *Luamar* and the *Hotel Vila Baleira*, this traditional stone building with a clay roof attracts a young clientele for drinks and snacks such as *chouriço* (sausage), *picado* (garlicky beef), *pregos* (beef in a roll) and *camarão* (shrimps). There's rock and pop music inside and a covered terrace outside.

Mercearia

Rua João Gonçalves Zarco 26, Vila Baleira. Daily 11am–2am. With palm-shaded tables in an attractive patio, this stone-walled bar is characterful and cool (literally and metaphorically). In summer, a little kiosk dispenses *poncha* in the garden.

Bar Taskaki

Rua João João Gonçalves Zarco, Vila Baleira Daily 8am–2am. A fashionable, loungey music bar just south of the old market building, with comfy sofas, minimalist decor, resident DJ and dance sounds nightly.

Clubs

Challenger Beach

Penedo do Sono. Daily 10pm–8am. The harbourside branch of Vila Baleira's main club has taken over as *the* place to go on the island, with dance sounds till dawn and a mean selection of drinks ranging from *batidinhas* (fruit shakes) to *caipirinhas*.

Essentials

Arrival

Most visitors arrive at Madeira airport, some 18km to the east of the capital, Funchal. There are regular connections from the airport to Porto Santo (see below).

Madeira

If you're arriving on a package then you'll probably have a free transfer to your hotel from the airport. Otherwise, the Aerobus (Mon–Sat roughly hourly 9.30am–9.15pm, return 8.30am–8.15pm; €4, free to TAP passengers; 25min) runs to Funchal's seafront and the Hotel Zone. Local SAM **buses** #20, #53, #78, #156 also do the run but take up to twice as long. The SAM bus terminal is on Avenida Calouste Gulbenkian, from where it's just ten minutes' walk to the tourist office (see p.194). A **taxi** from the airport to Funchal takes twenty minutes and costs €20–30.

By car, take the fast airport road, which skirts round the northern upper slopes of the city and follow signs to central Funchal (signed *Centro*). For the Hotel Zone, follow signs to *Funchal Oeste*.

Porto Santo

There are regular fifteen-minute TAP Air Portugal **flights** from Madeira airport every one to two hours (☏ 291 520 821, Ⓦ www.tap.pt; around €150 return). There are no buses from Porto Santo's airport, but plenty of taxis and you'll only pay about €7 for the ten-minute trip into Vila Baleira, the capital.

The Porto Santo Ferry Line (☏ 291 210 300, Ⓦ www.portosantoline.pt) runs a daily **ferry** from Funchal harbour to Porto de Abrigo (Sat–Thurs 8am, Fri 7pm; no Tues sailings Jan–March & Oct–Dec; €50 return; 2hr 15min). Arrive at the ferry terminal at least thirty minutes before departure. Large items of luggage can be left on the numbered palettes next to the ferry entrance; remember the number and retrieve the luggage yourself at the other end. Connecting buses from Porto de Abrigo to Vila Baleira take five minutes (€1.40), while a taxi costs around €5. Ferries return to Funchal at various times between 6pm and 10.30pm depending on the month and day.

You can also visit the island on a day-trip "cruise", with or without a round of golf; return prices cost €83/54 (Oct–April) or €91/62 (May–Sept) with/without golf.

Transport

Madeira and Porto Santo both have an efficient bus network and taxis are relatively inexpensive. But if you're planning to get off the beaten track, you're going to have to either rent a car or take a tour.

Madeira

Although distances on the island are short, many of the roads are narrow and winding, so journeys can take time; nevertheless, even Porto Moniz, at the furthest point of the island, is less than two hours from Funchal.

Buses

Madeira's buses serve almost e village on the island from Fun various privately run bus ter **Tickets** are inexpensive – a Funchal to Porto Moniz,

Bus companies

The area in and around Funchal is served by the yellow Horários do Funchal (☏ 291 705 555, ⓦ www.horasiosdofunchal.pt). Generally the west and northwest of the island is served by Rodoeste Buses (☏ 291 2??)48, ⓦ www.rodoeste.pt), which leave from Rua Ribeira João Gomes, Funchal. The east and northeast of the island, including the airport, is served by SAM Buses (☏ 291 201 150) from Rua Calouste Gulbenkian, Funchal. Two smaller companies – Empresa de Automóveis do Caniço (to Caniço; ☏ 291 222 558) and Companhia dos Carros de São Gonçalo (to Camacha, Santo do Serra, the north and Curral das Freiras; ☏ 291 705 555) have their terminals on the Zona Velha end of Avenida do Mar in Funchal.

northeast of the island, costs around €7. Tickets can be bought on board from the conductor on all buses. Full timetables can be purchased from the main tourist office in Funchal, or visit ⓦ www.Madeira-island.com/bus_services.

Though reliable, the buses are geared to the needs of local people, so that day-trips are not always feasible, especially as many routes are slow and circuitous. It's also worth noting that buses don't serve much of the island's best scenic and walking territory, so it's worth renting a car. Details of **buses from Funchal** to specific places on the island are given in the guide. From villages outside Funchal, look for timetables at bus stops marked *paragem*, or ask in the local café.

Car rental

Madeira's size means that nowhere is too far to visit on a day-trip from Funchal by **car**. An ambitious EU-funded tunnelling programme has greatly reduced journey times with a network of underground dual carriageways, though it's worth taking some of the old, winding roads for a chance to see more of the landscape. It's also worth getting hold of a good map, however, as road signs are biased in favour of the new highway.

Rental prices are around €75 a day or €200 a week. Third-party insurance is usually included in the price, though fuller insurance is recommended to cover hefty excess charges for damages. insurance4carhire.com offers cheap annual excess cover. Petrol around €1.40 a litre.

To rent a car, you'll need a current driving licence from your home country or an international driving licence – as well as your passport, which you must have with you at all times when driving.

Parking is easy outside Funchal and Machico, where it's best to head for central car parks or try and find blue pay-and-display bays. Prices for these start at around €0.50 an hour, usually on *dias utéis* (weekdays) only. In other towns parking isn't usually a problem.

Car rental companies

Auto-Jardim Rua Ivens 12, Funchal ☏ 291 213 100; airport ☏ 291 524 023, ⓦ www.autocarhire.net.
Avis Largo António Nobre 164, Funchal ☏ 291 764 546; *Hotel Monumental Lido*, Funchal ☏ 291 764 546; airport ☏ 291 524 392, ⓦ www.avis.com.
Bravacar Caminho do Amparo 2, Funchal ☏ 291 764 400.
Hertz Centro Comercial Monumental Lido Loja 1, Estrada Monumental 284, Funchal ☏ 291 764 410; airport ☏ 291 523 040, ⓦ www.hertz.com.
Europcar, Estrada Monumental 306, Funchal ☏ 291 765 116; airport ☏ 291 524 633, ⓦ www.europcar.co.uk.
Lidorent Edifício Alto Lido, Estrada Monumental, Funchal ☏ 291 761 420, ☏ 291 761 635.
Moinho Estrada Monumental 28, Funchal ☏ 291 762 123, Porto Santo airport ☏ 291 982 780, ⓦ www.moinho -rentacar.com.
Rodavante Edifício Baía, Estrada Monumental, Funchal ☏ 291 758 506; airport ☏ 291 524 718, ⓦ www.rodavente.com.
Sixt Estrada Monumental 182, Funchal ☏ 291 764 221, ⓦ www.e-sixt.com.

Taxis

If you don't fancy driving yourself, it's worth considering hiring a **taxi** for a day or half-day tour to any part of the island, or for local runs (to the start of walks, for example). Most authorized taxi drivers speak good English and can be extremely knowledgeable as guides. The tourist office in Funchal can book taxi tours in advance at set rates. If you want to book your own driver, call ☎91 873 6563. Make sure you agree a price beforehand. Prices run around €80–150 for a full day.

Motorbikes and bikes

Motorbikes are an excellent way of getting round the island and the narrow streets of central Funchal, though you'll need to rent a machine of above 100cc to be able to negotiate the mountainous interior. Prices start at around €25 a day. You'll need to be over 21, hold a valid **driving licence** from your home country or an international driving licence, and your passport. You must keep these at all times when you are driving. A hefty security deposit is also usually required. Wearing a **helmet** is obligatory; these come as part of the bike rental. Try **Joyride** (Centro Comercial Olimpo, Loja 210, Avenida do Infante, Funchal ☎291 234 906, ⓦwww .madeiramotorbikes.com), which also rents out **mountain bikes** (around €11 a day) and scooters (€20).

Tours

Most major hotels and travel agents can arrange well-organized and informative island-wide **sightseeing coach tours**, usually with a daily changing programme. One good-value option is Strawberry World, Centro Comercial Monumental Lido, Estrada Monumental, Funchal ☎291 762 429, ⓦwww .strawberry-world.com, which can also arrange spectacular **helicopter tours**. Ten to thirty-minute rides depart from just below Parque da Santa Catarina in Funchal (☎291 232 882 for details).

In Funchal, Carristur (☎966 923 943) offers hop-on hop-off open-top **bus tours** of the town (daily every 30min 9.30am–5.30pm; €10), taking in most of the main sights.

Porto Santo

Six **bus** routes, operated by Horários de Transportes, run round the island serving most sights – details are given in the text – but they're geared up to the needs of locals rather than tourists, so you may have to hang around for return buses. **Taxis** are relatively inexpensive; a ride from one end of the island to the other costs around €20, except during weekends and at night when tariffs double. The main taxi rank in Vila Baleira is on Rua Manuel G Pestana Junior (☎291 982 123).

Car rental is available at the airport from Moinho (see listings opposite). You can rent scooters from Acessórios Colombo, near the campsite on Avenida Henrique Vieira de Castro 64, Vila Baleira (☎291 984 438) for around €30 a day, or **bikes** from €10 a day. Both are a good way of getting up and down the flat coast road; bicycles are also rented out to non-residents by all the large hotels.

A slower but more traditional form of transport is the covered **carriola**, a colourful pony and trap that can be hired from the harbour or at the junction of Avenida Dr Manuel Gregório Pestana Júnior and Avenida Infante Dom Henrique in Vila Baleira. Rides start from €20 for half an hour, or €30 for an hour.

Tours

An open-top bus, run by Moinho (☎291 982 780), does a daily two-hour circuit of the island, leaving at 2pm from the petrol station outside the Pingo Doce in Vila Baleira (minimum of five people; €6 per person), with stops in Fonte D'Areia, Pico Castelo and Portela. Dunas (☎291 983 088, ⓔdunastravel@mail .telepac.pt) also offers island tours (3hr) from €18 per person, along with jeep safaris from €23 and walks, usually to the western peaks, from €15 (minimum six people).

Accommodation

Most of Madeira's hotels are first rate: the majority are four-star rated or over, with page-long lists of facilities. If you want a top-end hotel, it's usually cheaper to book one as part of a package tour, but if you're travelling independently, you'll find a good range of options, from hotels and guesthouses (called *pensão* or *residencial*) to rural quintas (manor houses). Villas are relatively scarce, though self-catering rooms with kitchenettes are available at many of the bigger hotels. **Camping** is limited to one site in the north (see p.158) and another on Porto Santo (see p.186), though it's possible to camp in restricted areas with prior permission; ⓦ www .madeira-camping.com can arrange this.

Accommodation prices given in the guide are for the **cheapest double room** in peak-season (Easter and mid-July to early Sept), though at New Year rates rocket and a minimum stay may be required: it's best to book well in advance over this period. At other times, prices can fall dramatically. Most hotels offer a fifty-percent reduction for children aged 2–12, and under-2s are usually free.

Unless otherwise stated, breakfast is included in the price at all the places listed in the guide.

Quintas, inns, country houses, youth hostels and rooms

Before *Reid's* became Funchal's first purpose-built hotel, visitors to the island were put up at wealthy landowners' estates, known as **quintas**. Nowadays many of these quintas have been adapted to offer characterful, hotel-style accommodation once more, sometimes in the original buildings or in modern extensions. Again, amenities tend to be first rate, with many having pools and lush grounds.

Away from Funchal and the main towns you can also find quality accommodation in rural areas in **estalagems** or **albergarias** – literally "inns" – which have similar facilities to quintas. Another option is staying in farms or rural houses on a **bed-and-breakfast** basis. These are known as *Turismo no Espaço Rural* or *casas rural* (ⓦ www.madeira-rural .com); most offer meals and some also have self-catering facilities. You'll almost certainly need a car to reach these places, however.

There are also a handful of small, inexpensive **youth hostels**. Non-YHA-members can join at reception for a small fee. For full details visit ⓦ www .pousadasjuventude.pt.

In many of Madeira's smaller towns you will see signs advertising **quartos** or **dormidas** – private rooms in people's houses, which can also be good value, though most don't offer breakfast. Try asking at the local café.

Information

The main Madeira **tourist office** is in Funchal on Avenida Arriaga 16 (Mon–Fri 9am–8pm, Sat & Sun 9am–6pm; ☎291 211 902). Tourist offices throughout the island (listed in the guide) and most major hotels give out free **maps** of Madeira and the main towns, which are adequate for basic touring. For in-depth exploration, the best road map is the GeoCentre's 1:75,000 *Holiday Map, Madeira*, which includes Porto Santo, although even this may not show the newest sections of Madeira's ongoing road-building programme.

Most **European newspapers** arrive in Madeira on the day of publication. For upcoming events, try and get hold of *Agenda Cultural*, an excellent monthly listings magazine available from the tourist office and some hotels.

Madeira on the net

Ⓦ **www.madeiraonline.com**. The main Madeira search engine, with links to countless other sites covering everything from walks to news, recipes, arts and education.
Ⓦ **www.madeira-portugal.com**. Website promoting hotels on Madeira, with details of facilities and prices and pictures of the hotels themselves. Also car rental and tours.

Ⓦ **www.madeira-holiday.com**. Well-designed and highly readable Net magazine run by the newspaper *Madeira Life*, with local news, features, good links and practical details.
Ⓦ **www.madeiratourism.org**. The snazzy official tourist board site, offering general information and hotel contact details.
Ⓦ **www.madeira-island.com**. Lively Net magazine with stacks of information on local news and events as well as details of accommodation, shops, bus times, car rental, and so on.
Ⓦ **www.madeira-shopping.com**. Chance to buy Madeiran produce online, with everything from books, guide books and maps to cakes, CDs and wine.

Money

As many products need to be imported, Madeira is more expensive than mainland Portugal, but food, drink and entry to sights remain relatively inexpensive.

The currency is the **euro** (€). The easiest way to get money is to use a credit or debit card to withdraw cash from any of the large number of **ATMs** (signed *Multibanco*) found throughout the island. Any card using the Cirrus system will work, as will all major credit cards (Visa, American Express, Mastercard and Eurocard). Credit and charge cards levy a fee of around three to four percent on any cash advance or purchase; for debit cards there is a small currency conversion fee and most

banks also charge per transaction. Credit cards are accepted for payment in most hotels and restaurants. It's very expensive to change **traveller's cheques** (up to €13 a transaction) although it's probably worth taking a supply in case you lose your credit card.

Normal **banking hours** are Mon–Fri 8.30am–2.45pm. In Funchal, some banks also open on Sat 9am–1pm. Currency exchange bureaux (*cambios*) generally open Mon–Fri 9am–1pm & 2–7pm, Sat 9am–7pm. Outside these hours, most major hotels offer currency exchange, though not always at favourable rates.

Food

Madeira does not share the culinary heritage of mainland Portugal, traditionally relying on local produce: namely maize, chicken, pork, beef, limpets, octopus and fish, especially tuna and the deep-sea *espada*

(scabbard fish), similar in taste to a delicate cod. Local restaurants are best, serving simply cooked, fresh produce such as beef kebabs, tuna with onions, limpet rice or *espada* with banana, often with delicious *bolo do caco* garlic bread or tasty fried maize. Sadly many establishments endeavour to cater to northern European tastes with unnecessary sauces and overboiled vegetables. Most restaurants also serve a range of international dishes, while Italian, Chinese and Indian restaurants can be found throughout Funchal. Look out too for some great desserts, especially those featuring the local fruits such as passion or kiwi fruit.

Menus are generally in Portuguese with an English translation. Most restaurants **open** for lunch from around noon until 3pm and for dinner from around 7pm to 11pm. Some close one day during the week.

The average **price** for a main course with cover and wine is around €20 per person. Anything much less than this is described in the guide as inexpensive; anything over €20, as expensive.

Sport and outdoor activities

With its wide open spaces and extensive coastline, Madeira is perfect for outdoor enthusiasts year-round, and there are countless activities that can be enjoyed either individually or as part of a group.

Walking

Some of the best walks on the island are detailed in this guide. These were accurate when the book went to press, but conditions change – landslides during the winter months can wipe out sections of path, as can road-building – so check that the walk is still manageable with the local tourist office or your hotel before you set off.

The best walking months are usually July, August and early September, when rain is uncommon and skies are generally

Levadas

The most famous walking trails on Madeira are along the concrete or stone sides of the island's **levadas** – irrigation canals constructed to channel water from the mountains to lower-lying agricultural land. Some of the *levadas* have been hacked into the side of sheer-sided slopes, and they often run through tunnels. Initially the work was done by slaves imported from Portugal's former colonies in Africa; nowadays high-tech machinery does the job. They have been constructed with an astonishing degree of engineering accuracy, along carefully plotted gradients so that the water flows gently down to where it is needed. Water flow is carefully regulated by a system of sluices operated by the *levadeiros* – men whose job it is to ensure that different farmers get an equal amount of water to their land and who keep the *levadas* clean and flowing.

As well as bringing water to farmers, the canals have proved to be ideal walkways, with a network of over 2000km winding across the island at gentle gradients. These, along with *veredas* – footpaths – are big business, with several tour companies offering guided walks. Though this has had the inevitable effect of removing the solitude from some of the walks, it has had the advantage of encouraging the local government to improve signposting and to provide dangerous sections with new fencing.

clear – and high up, at least, it's not too hot. June is the month most likely to have cloud covering the coasts, while the rainier months can make *levada* paths slippery. At other times, clouds often form over the mountains in the afternoons, so an early start is recommended.

All the walks in this guide can be tackled by anyone who is averagely fit, but make sure you're properly prepared. Some paths cross precipitous terrain and weather conditions can change quickly, reducing visibility and making the paths extremely slippery. Always wear suitable footwear and take a torch, suncream and waterproofs.

If you're unsure about setting off on a walk alone, consider taking a **guided walk**, such as those offered by Madeira Explorers (see below). Most hotels organize a weekly walking programme, and the companies listed below offer half- or full-day walks, with prices starting at around €25 for a half day to €40 for full-day tours. The price includes pick-up and drop off at your hotel.

Walking tour operators

Madeira Explorers ☎291 763 701 ⓦwww.Madeira-explorers.com.
MB Tours ☎291 203 950, ⓦwww.mb-travel.com.
Natura Travel ☎291 775 882, ⓦwww.madeirawalks.com.
Turitrans (Caniço de Baixo) ☎291 935 532, ⓦwww.turitrans-infocentre.com.

Cycling and adventure sports

With its arduous gradients and narrow roads, Madeira doesn't lend itself to casual cycling. However, it is possible to cycle along some footpaths and *levadas*, as well as across the Paúl da Serra inland plain.

A good way to see some of the best of the island is to take a half- or full-day organized mountain-bike tour. Tours (around €35–40) can be arranged by Terras de Aventura (☎291 776 818, ⓦwww.terrasdeaventura.com); they also offer canyoning, kayaking and watersports. The

relatively flat island of Porto Santo is much more cycle-friendly and nearly all the main hotels rent out bikes.

Diving

Many of the larger hotels on Madeira can arrange scuba diving, usually in the protected waters around Garajau and Caniço de Baixo, or off Machico. Porto Santo also has good diving, especially dives to the *Madeirense*, an old ferry which sunk south of the harbour in 2000. For more challenging dives, you'll need to show a diving certificate and logbook. Basic equipment hire starts at around €25 per day. Most places also arrange four- to five-day PADI diving courses for beginners for around €350–450. Once in the sea, you can swim face to face with moray eels, conger eels, squid, octopus, monkfish, tuna, parrot fish, mantas and Atlantic rays.

Diving centres

Baleira Diving *Hotel Vila Baleira*, Porto Santo ☎912 240 548.
Madeira Ocenas *Hotel Dom Pedro Baia*, Machico ☎968 052 543, ⓔbaleia@mail.telepac.pt.
Manta Diving Centre *Lido Galomar*, Caniço de Baixo ☎291 935 588, ⓦwww.mantadiving.com.

Surfing and other watersports

Madeira was discovered as a surfing destination by Portuguese and Brazilian surfers during the 1990s, and now hosts annual surfing championships – usually in January or February in Jardim do Mar and in Paúl do Mar in September. Madeira's deep Atlantic waters supply superb breakers, and the main attraction is the challenge of the big riders – three-metre-high waves which crash onto the basalt rock of the sea bed; extreme care and skill is required. As yet, there is no local surfing association and no surf shops on Madeira – some see this as local government reluctance to embrace surfers, a view fuelled by the recent construction of sea walls whose backwash has spoiled some surfing conditions. Surfers are advised to take their own board repair kits. Further information can be found on ⓦwww.wannasurf.com.

The Atlantic also offers ideal conditions for **windsurfing** – a native Madeiran won the 1996 World Windsurfing Championship – and many of the major hotels in Funchal rent out windsurfing equipment. Praia Formosa is a good place to try it, with equipment hire from €15 an hour. This is also the best place to hire **jet-skis** and **waterskis**, or contact Terras de Aventura (☎291 776 818, ⓦwww.terrasdeaventura.com).

Boat trips, sea fishing and dolphin watching

There are countless boat trips on offer from Funchal harbour, from simple cruises to dolphin watching and fishing – you can even tour on a replica of Christopher Columbus' galleon, the *Santa Maria de Colombo* (☎291 220 327). Two- to three-hour trips start at around €25. Historically, Madeira had a flourishing whaling industry, but now whaling is prohibited and its waters offer a safe haven for sea mammals. **Whales** rarely go near Funchal's coastline, though they can occasionally be seen in deeper water, while **dolphins** are far more common closer to the shore.

The 23-metre catamaran *Sea Born* (☎ 291 231 312, ⓦ www.seaborn.pt.vu) offers dolphin watching for around €30. Similar trips are offered on the yachts *Ventura do Mar* (☎291 280 033, ⓦwww.venturadomar.com) and *Gavião* (☎291 241 124, ⓔgaviaomadeira@netmadeira.com), which also runs trips to the neighbouring Ilhas Desertas for around €80.

The deep off-shore waters around the island offer some of the world's best **big game fishing**, especially for Atlantic blue marlin, which can weigh over 1000lbs (in

season June–Sept). Other fish include blue eye tuna (June–Sept), blue shark, hammerhead shark, barracuda, bonito and wahoo (April–Oct), and Manta rays (Aug–Oct). Various fishing operators operate from Funchal marina.

Fishing trip operators

Katherine B Marina do Funchal, Funchal ☎291 752 685, ⓦwww.fishmadeira.com.
Nautisantos Rua Dr A. J. da Oliveira 2, Funchal ☎291 231 312, ⓦwww.nautisantosfishing.com.
Xiphias Sport Fishing Marina do Funchal, Funchal, ☎291 289 007 ⓦwww.xiphias.no.sapo.pt.

Football

Madeira's top sides are Funchal-based Marítimo (ⓦ www.csmaritimo.pt) and Nacional (ⓦwww.nacional.novamadeira.com), who both play in the top Portuguese league and entertain top sides like Porto and Benfica.

Traditionally the more successful of the two sides, Marítimo play at the ageing **Barreiros Stadium** on Rua do Dr Pita in Funchal (☎291 205 000), though they are due to move to a new Estádio do Marítimo in Praia Formosa by 2008-2009 (see p.74). Nacional, who finished a record-high fourth in 2003–2004, play in the Estádio E Rui Alves in Choupana (☎291 223 855). Tickets can be bought for most matches from the stadiums, or in advance from the club shops in Funchal (Nacional: Rua do Esmeraldo 46; Marítimo: Rua Dom Carlos 14, see p.90).

Tennis

Most of the major hotels have their own tennis courts. In Funchal, there are public courts at Quinta Magnolia on Dr Pita (see p.71; daily 8am–9pm; ☎291 763 237) while Porto Santo has top facilities at the **Porto Santo Tennis Academy** (Estrada da Calheta, Campo de Baixo ☎291 983 274, ⓔgoldentenis@mail.pt), a top-notch complex which hosts occasional tournaments and lets out courts from €10 an hour.

Horse riding

Madeira is too hilly for decent horse riding, though you can trek from Porto Santo's Centro Hípico (riding centre; ☎ 291 983 258), which offers fifty-minute treks for around €25.

Golf

Madeira boasts two quality golf courses in spectacular locations: Santo da Serra (see p.130), which hosts the Madeira Open in March, and Palheiro Golf (see p.101). Inexperienced golfers can have lessons at either course, though only the latter allows inexperienced golfers onto the greens. If you plan to play a lot of golf, it's worth asking the clubs for the names of hotels whose guests get a discount on green fees. Porto Santo also has a highly rated course (see p.181). Details of the courses are given in the guide, or see ⓦ www.Madeira-golf.com.

Children's Madeira

Recommended attractions for children include the water slides in the Aqua Parque near Santa Cruz (see p.117), the Parque Temático in Santana (see p.166), the toboggan ride in Monte (see p.97) and the various cable cars in Monte, Santana, Garajau, Cabo Girão and Achada da Cruz. Porto Moniz is a particularly good family destination thanks to its aquarium, Centro de Ciência Viva science centre and sea pools, while Madeira Magic in Funchal (see p.74) is a good wet-weather attraction for younger kids.

The larger package hotels generally have good facilities for children, though it's worth establishing what is available before you book. Many places have children's swimming pools, play areas and – for older kids – games rooms. Some hotels also offer babysitting and the smarter ones have creche facilities and special kids' programmes.

Note that fresh milk – leite do dia – can usually only be bought from larger supermarkets. Smaller shops tend to stock only long-life milk. International-brand baby foods, formula milk, nappies and baby products are all widely available in supermarkets and chemists.

Holidays and festivals

Madeira has a good share of public holidays, during which banks and most shops close and buses operate to a Sunday timetable. However, most tourist services – including cafés, restaurants and sites – function as normal.

Madeira also has a seemingly endless supply of festivals, which crop up all over the island – the biggest and best of them are listed below. See also p.28.

Festivals

January
Night Festival and End of New Year Festivities (January 6). The official end of

Public holidays

1 January	5 October Republic Day
25 April Revolution Day	1 November All Saints' Day
1 May Labour Day	1 December Independence Day
10 June Portugal/Camões Day	8 December Immaculate Conception
1 July Discovery of Madeira Day	25 December
15 August Assumption	

the New Year's festivities, with live music and dance in Funchal and elsewhere.

February–March

Carnival festivities in Funchal (see box on p.59).

April–May

Festa da Flor Three-day flower festival in Funchal. Main events include the Wall of Hope Ceremony in Praça do Município, in which children pin posies onto the city hall and make a wish, and a parade the following day.

June

Santos Populares (Popular Saints). June sees the celebration of the main saints' days:

St Anthony, the patron saint of lovers (June 13). Evening festivities include the tradition of jumping over fires (it is said that the highest leapers will be lucky in love).

St John (June 24) is the big saint's day for Funchal, with shops competing to prepare the most lavishly decorated mock altar. Evening festivities centre on Largo do Carmo, with similar events in Porto Santo.

St Peter (June 29), the patron saint of fishermen, celebrated most enthusiastically in the fishing ports of Câmara de Lobos and in Ribeira Brava.

Classic Car Rally Some 60 vehicles dating back to the 1920s tour round the island, starting and finishing in Funchal.

Madeira Music Festival Various concerts and performances throughout the island, many accompanied by fireworks.

July

Dança de 24 horas Various folk dancing groups gather in Santana to perform over a riotous 24-hour period – and sometimes longer – with food and drink stalls to help keep them going.

Funchal Jazz Festival Live jazz performed in the capital, mostly in the gardens of Quinta Magnolia.

August

Madeira Wine Rally (first weekend, Ⓦ www.ralivm.com) International amateur rally drivers speed round the island's precipitous roads in what is considered one of most challenging rallies in Europe.

Festival of the Assumption (August 15) Island-wide celebrations. The biggest is at Nossa Senhora do Monte in Monte (Aug 14–15).

Festa do Santissimo Sacramento (Festival of the Holy Sacrament; last Sun of Aug) A carnival-style procession departs from Machico, culminating in a huge bonfire on the neighbouring Pico de Facho.

September

Nossa Senhora da Piedade (third Sun) A statue of the Virgin is taken from a chapel in the cliffs above Prainha to Caniçal by fishermen in a procession of boats.

Madeira Wine Festival The wine harvest is celebrated with barefoot grape-treading and folk dancing in Estreito de Câmara de Lobos, at Quinta Furão (near Santana), and with special shows and exhibitions in Funchal. There's also a Grape Festival in Porto da Cruz.

Colombus Week Three days' festivities in honour of Christopher Colombus on Porto Santo (see box on p.182).

Festa de Senhor Jesus Religious festival in Ponta Delgada when a holy relic is paraded round the village (see p.160).

November

Festa das Castanhas (Chestnut Festival) Folk displays and chestnut dishes are dished up in Curral das Freiras to celebrate the local harvest.

International Film Festival Funchal's Baltazar Dias theatre on Avenida Arriaga (☎291 226 371) hosts a range of the best films from around the world.

Christmas build up Spectacular Christmas lights are turned on in Funchal in mid-November.

December

Christmas On December 16, traditional nativity scenes are set up. For locals, the main event is on December 24, with Midnight Mass followed by a traditional meal of *bacalhau*. On Christmas Day, most hotels lay on special Christmas meals and events.

New Year's Eve Funchal has a justifiable reputation as one of the best places in the world to see in the New Year. Virtually every house in the city puts on all its lights, the harbour is jammed with visiting cruise liners, and at midnight the whole bay becomes a riot of blasting ships' sirens and exploding fireworks – the jamboree of 2006 was officially the largest firework display in the world. It is traditional to see in the New Year with *bolo de mel* and champagne. Be aware that many hotels have obligatory New Year's Eve "gala" dinners at stonking rates, which can cost over €100 per person – check to see what you're tied to before you book.

Directory

Addresses These follow the Portuguese convention of having the street name followed by the building number. A number followed by, for example, 4° shows it is on the fourth floor. In smaller villages the address may have no street name, or with a general area name such as *Sítio da Igreja*, roughly meaning "in the place where the church is".

Airlines TAP Air Portugal, Avda do Mar 10 and airport (☎291 520 821); British Airways, airport (☎291 520 870); easyJet (www.easyjet.com); GB Airways, airport (☎291 524 539).

Airport information ☎291 220 064 (Madeira); ☎291 980 120 (Porto Santo); ✪www.anam.pt.

Clothes Though Madeira is warm all year, take a warm top for the cooler evenings and for visiting the mountains. A light raincoat is also recommended year-round.

Consulates Britain, Rua da Alfandega 10, 3°, Funchal ☎291 221 860; USA, Rua da Alfandega 10, 2°, Funchal ☎291 235 636.

Electricity The current is 220 volts AC. Most sockets take two-point round pins as in continental Europe. UK appliances work with an adaptor, but North American appliances will also need a transformer.

Emergencies Call ☎112 for police, ambulance or fire brigade.

gay scene Most of the island has a conservative attitude to homosexuality, though in Funchal people are more open-minded. Its annual carnival kicks off with a transvestite night, and though there are no specific bars or clubs for gays, *Café do Teatro* (see p.67) is a popular gay hangout.

Hospital Hospital Cruz Carvalho, Av Luís Camões, Funchal (☎291 705 600). Most villages – and Porto Santo – also have a Centro da Saúde (health centre) for basic care.

Internet Most major hotels have modem points and much of the island is a Wi-Fi zone. Most hotels and post offices also have terminals you can use, as do Internet cafés in the larger towns.

Lost property Rua Infância

Pharmacy For minor health complaints you should go to a *farmácia* (pharmacy), which you'll find in almost any village. Most have someone who can speak English. The pharmacists are trained to dispense suitable medication that would normally only be available on prescription in Britain or North America. Pharmacies are usually open Mon–Fri 9am–1pm & 3–7pm, Sat 9am–1pm. In the larger towns, they take it in turns to stay open out-of-hours (*fora das horas*); check in any pharmacy window for the address of the one which is open.

Phones Most UK, Australian and New Zealand mobile phones will work in Madeira, though US-bought handsets, which use a different system, may not. Check with your phone provider. Nearly all hotels have their own telephones, but these are invariably more expensive than public phones. It's best to make international calls using a *credifone*, a phone card which you can buy in denominations of €3, €6 or €9 from post offices, some newspaper kiosks and shops with a CTT sign. The main post offices also have pay cabins charging the same rate as a *credifone*; take a token from the attendant and pay for the call at the end. The cheap rate for international calls is between 10pm and 8am and at weekends.

Photography For digital or conventional film processing, try Belafoto at the Anadia Shopping Centre on Rua Visconde Anadia, just up from the main market.

Police To report a theft or any crime, go to the main station on Rua Infância 28 ☎ 291 208 200. On Porto Santo, the main police station is at Sítio das Matas in Vila Baleira ☎ 291 982 423.

Post office Funchal's main post office is on Avenida Calouste Gulbenkian 3, next to the SAM bus terminal (Mon–Fri 8.30am–6.30pm). The city's most central post office is on Avenida Zarco (Mon–Fri 8.30am–8pm, Sat 9am–1pm). The main post office in Porto Santo is on Avenida Vieira de Castro, Vila Baleira, opposite the tourist office (Mon–Fri 9am–6pm, Sat 9am–1pm).

Shopping Traditional shopping hours are Monday to Friday 9am–1pm & 3–7pm, Saturday 9am–1pm. Some shopping centres and tourist shops stay open for lunch and until 10pm Monday to Saturday.

Supermarkets Madeira's biggest and best supermarket is Pingo Doce. There are several branches round the town, such as opposite the Lido and at the Anadia Shopping Centre on Rua Visconde Anadia just up from the main market (open daily 9am–10pm). There are also branches in Machico, on Rua General António Teixeira de Aguiar and Vila Baleira on Porto Santo, on the junction of Av Dr Manuel Gregório Pestana Júnior and Rua Bartolomeu Perestrelo.

Time Madeira follows GMT (late Sept to late March) and BST (late March to late Oct). This is 5hr ahead of Eastern Standard Time and 8hr ahead of Pacific Standard Time.

Tipping Large tips are not expected – 10 percent will certainly suffice. Service charges are normally included in hotel and restaurant bills.

Toilets There are public toilets in most towns. You should tip attendants.

Water is safe to drink from a tap anywhere on the island, though on neighbouring Porto Santo it's best to stick to bottled water: as the tap water is desalinated, it tastes revolting. In theory, water in *levadas* is also safe to drink on the higher mountain slopes, but should definitely not be drunk lower down as it may have passed through farmland.

Chronology

Chronology

888,000 BC ▶ Madeira's turbulent volcanic activity ceases, resulting in a series of fertile peaks rising some 6000m above the bed of the Atlantic.

50–200 AD ▶ Greek and Roman scribes refer to Atlantic islands they call the "Red" and "Purple" Isles – suggesting they were aware of the red sap from Madeira's native dragon trees, formerly used for dye.

1346 ▶ Legend states that English merchant Robert Machin is shipwrecked at Machico. He escapes on a raft only to be captured by pirates and sold as a slave. His tale eventually reaches the Portuguese court, inspiring sailors to seek the mysterious island.

1418 ▶ João Gonçalves (aka 'Zarco') and Tristão Vaz Teixeira are sent by Henry the Navigator to explore the African coast. Blown off course, they shelter on Porto Santo but spot a densely wooded island they call *Ilha da Madeira* – Island of Wood.

1419 ▶ The sailors return to the islands with Bartolemeu Perestrello, who becomes governor of Porto Santo. Zarco and Teixeira land at Machico.

1425–40 ▶ The first colonizers settle on the islands, which are declared a province of Portugal, with the capital at Machico. Wheat and later sugar beet is planted in the fertile soil and slaves are imported to dig irrigation canals (*levadas*).

1478–97 ▶ Sugar trader Christopher Columbus settles on the islands after marrying Bartolemeu Perestrello's daugher. In 1497, Manuel I declares Funchal the capital.

1500–66 ▶ Flemish traders exchange works of art for sugar. The Sé (cathedral) is consecrated in 1516. Forts are built to defend the island from pirate attach. Nevertheless, in 1566, French pirates kill three hundred Madeirans during a sixteen-day rampage.

1581–1639 ▶ Philip II of Spain defeats rivals' claims to the Portuguese throne to become Felipe I of Portugal. In 1582, the new Spanish governor of Madeira builds the Fortaleza de São Tiago in Funchal and Pico do Castelo on Porto Santo. Madeiran timber is used to build the Spanish Armada.

1640 ▶ Portugal regains independence from Spain under João IV.

1658 ▶ With a floundering sugar trade and weakened global influence, the Portuguese woo the British by establishing the British Factory, giving British merchants favourable trading concessions in the growing wine trade.

1662 ▶ Britain's trading clout grows after Charles II marries Portugal's Catherine of Bragança. Madeira is almost given to the British as part of the dowry.

c18th ▶ Madeira flourishes as a major trading post. Wealthy British traders finance a British church, cemetery and hospital, though local Madeirans struggle to make ends meet.

1807–15 ▶ Several thousand British troops occupy the island after Napoleon invades mainland Portugal. Napoleon eventually calls on Madeira in 1815 – en route to exile in St Helena.

1815–52 ▶ Recession and crop-failures force the British Factory to close down. The island economy diversifies into banana cultivation, embroidery and basket-making. A cholera epidemic in 1852 causes mass emigration, mostly to Venezuela and South Africa.

1853–1900 ▶ Wealthy travellers – mostly Brits – begin to call on Madeira en route to overseas colonies. Reids opens in 1891 to cater to the growing tourism trade. A railway is built to link Funchal with holiday quintas in Monte.

1900–18 ▶ Germany becomes an important trading ally. When World War I breaks out, Madeira confiscates German property on the island at Britain's request. In retaliation, Funchal is twice bombarded by German submarines.

1932–70 ▶ Dr António Salazar rules Portugal with an iron fist. Madeiran uprisings in 1931 are swiftly snuffed out. The island is left to stagnate and poverty is rife. Wealthy tourists – including Churchill – visit Madeira by flying boat until an airport opens in Porto Santo in 1960, then in Madeira in 1964.

1974–86 ▶ Salazar's regime is overthrown in a revolution in 1974 and Madeira is declared an autonomous political region under Dr Alberto João Jardim. The economy begins to thrive.

1986 to present ▶ Entry into the EU sees funds pour into the island, leading to a radical road building programme, an expanded airport and corresponding boom in house building and tourism.

Language

Portuguese

English is widely spoken in the majority of Madeira's hotels and tourist restaurants, but you'll find a few words of Portuguese extremely useful if you are travelling on public transport, or in more out-of-the-way places. If you have some knowledge of Spanish, you won't have much problem reading Portuguese. Understanding it when it's spoken, though, is a another matter: pronunciation is entirely different and at first even the easiest words are hard to distinguish. Once you've started to figure out how words are pronounced it gets a lot easier very quickly.

A useful word is **há** (the H is silent), which means "there is" or "is there?" and can be used for just about anything. Thus: "*Há uma pensão aqui?*" (Is there a guesthouse here?) More polite and better in shops or restaurants are "**Tem**...?" (pronounced *taying*) which means "Do you have...?", or "**Queria**..." (I'd like...). And of course there are the old standards "Do you speak English?" (*Fala Inglês?*) and "I don't understand" (*Não compreendo*).

Pronunciation

The chief difficulty with **pronunciation** is its lack of clarity – consonants tend to be slurred, while vowels are nasal and often ignored altogether. The **consonants**, at least, are consistent:

C is soft before E and I, hard otherwise unless it has a cedilla – *açucar* (sugar) is pronounced "assookar".

CH is closer to *sh*; *chá* (tea) sounds like "shah".

J is pronounced like the "s" in pleasure. **G** is pronounced in the same way before "weak" vowels – *gelo* (ice) is pronounced "jelloo" – but like the English G before a "strong" vowels such as *geografia* (geography).

LH sounds like "lyuh" – *pilha* (battery) is pronounced "pillyuh".

Q is always pronounced as a "k" – *queimadas* (the name of a local area), for example, is pronounced "kay-madash'.

S before a consonant or at the end of a word becomes "sh", otherwise it's as in English – Sagres (a brand of beer) is pronounced "sahgresh".

X is also pronounced "sh"– *caixa* (cash desk) is pronounced "kaisha".

Vowels are worse – flat and truncated, they're often difficult for English-speaking tongues to get around. The only way to learn is to listen: accents, Ã, Ô or É, turn them into longer, more familiar sounds.

When two vowels come together they continue to be enunciated separately except in the case of EI and OU. The former sounds like a long "a" – *geladeira* (fridge) is pronounced "jeladaira" – and the latter like a long "o" – *outubro* (October) is pronounced "ootubroo". E at the end of a word is silent unless it has an accent, so that *carne* (meat) is pronounced "karn", while *café* sounds much as you'd expect. The tilde over Ã or Õ renders the pronunciation more nasal, so the ã in *irmã* (sister) is like the *a* in the word *sang*. More common is ÃO (as in *pão*, bread; *são*, saint; *limão*, lemon), which sounds something like a strangled yelp of "ow!" cut off in midstream.

Words and phrases

Essentials

sim; não	yes; no
olá; bom dia	hello; good morning
boa tarde/noite	good afternoon/night
adeus, até logo	goodbye, see you later
hoje; amanhã	today; tomorrow
por favor/se faz favor	please
tudo bem?	is everything all right?
está bem	it's all right/OK
obrigado/a*	thank you
onde; que	where; what
quando; porquê	when; why
como; quanto	how; how much
não sei	I don't know
sabe…?	do you know…?
pode…?	could you…?
desculpe; com licença	sorry; excuse me
este/a; esse/a	this; that
agora; mais tarde	now; later
mais; menos	more; less
grande; pequeno	big; little
aberto; fechado	open; closed
senhoras; homens	women; men
lavabo/quarto de banho	toilet/bathroom

*Obrigado agrees with the sex of the person speaking – a woman says *obrigada*, a man *obrigado*.

Getting around

esquerda, direita,	left, right
sempre em frente	straight ahead
aqui; ali	here; there
perto; longe	near; far
Onde é…	Where is…
a estação	the bus sation
de camionetas?	
a paragem de autocarro para…	the bus stop for…
Donde parte o autocarro para…?	Where does the bus to… leave from?
A que horas parte?	What time does it leave?
(chega a…?)	(arrive at…?)
Pare aqui por favor	Stop here please
um bilhete (para)	a ticket (to)
ida e volta	round trip

Accommodation

Queria um quarto	I'd like a room
É para uma noite (semana)	It's for one night (week)
É para uma pessoa (duas pessoas)	It's for one person (two people)
Quanto custa?	How much is it?
Posso ver?	May I see/look around?
Há um quarto mais barato?	Is there a cheaper room?/
com uma vista	with a view (of the sea)?
com duche?	with a shower?

Shopping

Quanto é?	How much is it?
banco; câmbio	bank; change
correios	post office
(dois) selos	(two) stamps
para Reino Unido/Estados Unidos	for the UK/United States
Como se diz isto em Português?	What's this called in Portuguese?
O que é isso?	What's that?

Days of the week

domingo	Sunday
segunda-feira	Monday
terça-feira	Tuesday
quarta-feira	Wednesday
quinta-feira	Thursday
sexta-feira	Friday
sábado	Saturday

Numbers

um	1
dois	2
três	3
quatro	4
cinco	5
seis	6
sete	7
oito	8
nove	9
dez	10
onze	11
doze	12
treze	13
catorze	14
quinze	15
dezasseis	16
dezassete	17
dezoito	18
dezanove	19
vinte	20
vinte e um	21
trinta	30
quarenta	40
cinquenta	50
sessenta	60
setenta	70
oitenta	80
noventa	90
cem	100
cento e um	101
duzentos	200
quinhentos	500
mil	1000

Common Portuguese signs

Ar condicionado	air conditioned
Centro	(town) centre
Desvio	diversion (on road)
Dormidas	private rooms
Elevador	lift
Entrada	entrance
Fecha a porta	close the door
Incluído IVA	(price) includes VAT
Obras	roadworks
Paragem	bus stop
Perigo/Perigoso	danger/dangerous
Pré-pagamento	pay in advance
Proibido estacionar	no parking
Quartos	private rooms
Saida	exit
Turismo	tourist office

Menu glossary

Starters, staples and side dishes

arroz	rice
azeitonas	olives
batatas cozidas	boiled potatoes
batatas fritas	chips
fiambre	ham
legumes	vegetables
manteiga	butter
ovo (cozido)	(boiled) egg
pão	bread
pimenta	pepper
piri-piri	chilli sauce
presunto	smoked ham
queijo	cheese
sal	salt
salada (mista)	(mixed) salad
sopa de (peixe/canja/ legumes/tomate)	(fish/chicken/ vegetable/ tomato) soup

Meat

borrego	lamb
carne de porco	pork
carne de vaca	beef
coelho	rabbit
costeletas de porco	pork chops
dobrada/tripas	tripe
febras	pork steaks
fígado	liver
frango	young chicken
galinha	chicken
leitão	suckling pig
vitela	veal

Fish and seafood

atum	tuna
bodião	parrot fish
camarões	shrimps

Menu glossary **LANGUAGE**

caranguejo	crab
carapau	mackerel
chocos	cuttle fish
espada	scabbard fish
espadarte	swordfish
gambas	prawns
lagosta	lobster
lapas	limpets
linguada	sole
lulas	squid
pargo	sea bream
pescada	hake
polvo	octopus
salmão	salmon
salmonete	red mullet
sardinhas	sardines
truta	trout

Portuguese and Madeiran specialities

bacalhau à brás	salted cod with egg and potatoes
caldeirada	fish stew
cataplana	fish, shellfish or meat stewed in a circular metal dish
espada com banana/vinho e alhos	scabbard fish with banana/wine and garlic
espetada	kebab, usually beef
feijoada	bean casserole
milho frito	fried cornmeal
pão com alho/bolo do caco	garlic bread

Desserts (Sobremesa)

gelado	ice cream
maracuja	passion fruit
melão	melon
morangos	strawberries
pudim flan	crème caramel
salada da fruta	fruit salad
uvas	grapes

Other useful terms

almoço	lunch
cadeira	chair
colher	spoon
conta	the bill
copo	glass
ementa	menu
faca	knife
garfo	fork

jantar	dinner
mesa	table
pequeno almoco	breakfast
pimenta	pepper
quanto é?	how much is it?
quarto de banho	toilet
queria...	I'd like...
sal	salt

Cakes and snacks

bolos	cakes
bolo de mel	"honey cake" made of fruits, spices and molasses
pastéis de bacalhau	salted cod rissoles
pastéis de nata	custard-cream tarts
prego/bifana	garlic beef/ pork in a roll
rissois de camarão	fried shrimp puffs
sandes	sandwich
sandes de fiambre/ queijo/mista	ham/cheese/mixed sandwich

Coffee, tea and soft drinks

água (sem/com gás)	mineral water (without/with gas)
brisa maracujá	fizzy passion fruit juice
sumo de laranja/ maçã	orange/apple juice
chá	tea
café	coffee
sem/com leite	without/with milk
sem/com açúcar	without/with sugar
uma bica	a small, strong espresso

Alcoholic drinks

um copo/uma garrafa de/da	a glass/bottle of …
aguardente	firewater distilled from sugar cane
poncha aguardente	mixed with brandy, lemon and honey
licor de castanha	a distillation of the local chestnuts
sidra	cider
vinho branco/tinto	white/red wine
cerveja	beer
um imperial	a half glass
uma caneca	a large glass (half-litre)

Quinta Mãe dos Homens Funchal...

...your room with a view!

Quinta Mãe dos Homens offers you spectacular views
of Funchal and the Bay beyond.
Concealed within the Quintas eight acre grounds
you will find 24 self catering Studios, one bedroom
apartments and family Villas, all with a
private terrace or balcony.
At the hart of the Quinta you have the Clubhouse
and it secluded terrace overlooking the spacious
swimming pool and the Bay of Funchal beyond.

**Quinta Mãe dos Homens
One of the finest self catering holidays in Madeira.**

Visit our web site at www.qmdh.com
For further information please contact reservations on
+351 291 204410 or e-mail. quinta.mdh@netmadeira.com

Visit us online
www.roughguides.com

Information on over 25,000 destinations around the world

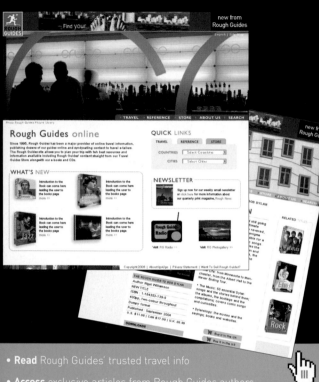

- **Read** Rough Guides' trusted travel info

- **Access** exclusive articles from Rough Guides authors

- **Update** yourself on new books, maps, CDs and other products

- **Enter** our competitions and win travel prizes

- **Share** ideas, journals, photos & travel advice with other users

- **Earn** points every time you contribute to the Rough Guide
  community and get rewards

BROADEN YOUR HORIZONS

small print & Index

SMALL PRINT

A Rough Guide to Rough Guides

In 1981, Mark Ellingham, a recent graduate in English from Bristol University, was travelling in Greece on a tiny budget and couldn't find the right guidebook. With a group of friends he wrote his own guide, combining a contemporary, journalistic style with a practical approach to travellers' needs. That first Rough Guide was a student scheme that became a publishing phenomenon. Today, Rough Guides include recommendations from shoestring to luxury and cover hundreds of destinations around the globe, including almost every country in the Americas and Europe, more than half of Africa and most of Asia and Australasia. Millions of readers relish Rough Guides' wit and inquisitiveness as much as their enthusiastic, critical approach and value-for-money ethos. The guides' ever-growing team of authors and photographers is spread all over the world.

In the early 1990s, Rough Guides branched out of travel, with the publication of Rough Guides to World Music, Classical Music and the Internet. All three have become benchmark titles in their fields, spearheading the publication of a range of more than 350 titles under the Rough Guide name, including phrasebooks, waterproof maps, music guides from Opera to Heavy Metal, reference works as diverse as Conspiracy Theories and Shakespeare, and popular culture books from iPods to Poker. Rough Guides also produce a series of more than 120 World Music CDs in partnership with World Music Network.

Visit www.roughguides.com to see our latest publications.

Rough Guide travel images are available for commercial licensing at www.roughguidespictures.com

Publishing information

This second edition published June 2008 by
Rough Guides Ltd, 80 Strand, London WC2R 0RL.
345 Hudson St, 4th Floor, New York,
NY 10014, USA.

Distributed by the Penguin Group
Penguin Books Ltd, 80 Strand, London WC2R 0RL
Penguin Group (USA), 375 Hudson Street,
NY 10014, USA
14 Local Shopping Centre, Panchsheel Park,
New Delhi 110017, India
Penguin Group (Australia), 250 Camberwell Road,
Camberwell, Victoria 3124, Australia
Penguin Group (Canada), 10 Alcorn Avenue,
Toronto, ON M4V 1E4, Canada
Penguin Group (NZ), 67 Apollo Drive, Mairangi Bay,
Auckland 1310, New Zealand
Typeset in Bembo and Helvetica to an original
design by Henry Iles.
Cover concept by Peter Dyer.

Printed and bound in China
© Matthew Hancock 2008

No part of this book may be reproduced in any form without permission from the publisher except for the quotation of brief passages in reviews.
224pp includes index

A catalogue record for this book is available from the British Library

ISBN 978-1-85828-054-7

1   3   5   7   9   8   6   4   2

Help us update

We've gone to a lot of effort to ensure that the second edition of Madeira & Porto Santo DIRECTIONS is accurate and up-to-date. However, things change – places get "discovered", opening hours are notoriously fickle, restaurants and rooms raise prices or lower standards. If you feel we've got it wrong or left something out, we'd like to know, and if you can remember the address, the price, the phone number, so much the better.

Please send your comments with the subject line "Madeira & Porto Santo DIRECTIONS Update" to ✉mail@roughguides.com. We'll credit all contributions and send a copy of the next edition (or any other Rough Guide if you prefer) for the very best emails.

Have your questions answered and tell others about your trip at ✆community.roughguides.com

Rough Guide credits

Text editor: Gavin Thomas
Layout: Pradeep Thapliyal
Photography: Matthew Hancock
Cartography: Jai Prakash Mishra
Picture editor: Sarah Cummins

Proofreader: Amanda Jones
Production: Rebecca Short
Design: Henry Isles
Cover design: Chloë Roberts

The author

Freelance writer Matthew Hancock commutes regularly to Portugal and likes nothing better than putting on his boots to walk Madeira's *levadas*.

Now resident in Dorset, he is also author of *Algarve* and *Lisbon Directions* and co-author of the *Rough Guide to Portugal*.

Acknowledgements

Thanks to Jane Gordon, Marina at Quinta Mãe dos Homens, Joana Dias at the Madeira Tourist Board, Anne Morris at ICEP, Madeira Explorers and to everyone at Rough Guides, especially Gavin for

fine tuning, Andy for keeping tabs on things and Katie Lloyd-Jones for map suggestions. Special thanks to Amanda, Alex and Olivia for support while I'm away.

Readers' letters

Thanks to all the readers of the first edition who took the trouble to write in with comments and suggestions:

Gillian Collins, Ana Paula Costa, John and

Jacqueline Hindley, Richard N Maddern, Simon Neal, Anthony Stigter & Kathrin Richter, Eduardo Welsh, Claudia Vasconcelos.

Photo credits

All images © Rough Guides except the following:

Front cover: Agapanthus flowers near Serra de Agua © H P Merten/Photolibrary.com
Back cover: Ostkap Halbinsel, Madeira © Tips Images

p.13 Lorano to Machico walk © Matthew Hancock
p.14 Lift to Fajã das Padres © Matthew Hancock
p.15 Santa Maria de Columbo © Matthew Hancock
p.16 Mountain biking © Madeira Tourism
p.17 Diving © Madeira Tourism
p.17 Football match at Barreiros Stadium in Funchal, Madeira © AFP/Getty
p.17 Porto Santo Golf Course © Matthew Hancock
p.17 Surfing © Madeira Tourism
p.21 Prainha beach © Matthew Hancock
p.24 Museu de Arte Sacra © Madeira Tourism
p.28 Funchal New Year's Eve © Helena Smith
p.28 Madeira Wine Festival, Câmara de Lobos © Prisma Die-Agenteur/Powerstock

p.29 Carros Antigos vintage car © Madeira Tourism
p.29 Columbus week © Madeira Tourism
p.29 Festa da Flor, Funchal © Madeira Tourism
p.29 Funchal Carnival © Madeira Tourism
p.31 Funchal balloon © Matthew Hancock
p.35 Sir Winston Churchill and Lady Clementine at *Reid's* © *Reid's* hotel
p.41 *Luamar Hotel* swimming pool © Matthew Hancock
p.114 Picnic spot, Garajau © Matthew Hancock
p.120 Diving off Caniço de Baixo © Madeira Tourism
p.127 Museu da Baleira © Madeira Tourism
p.130 Clube de Golf Santo da Serra © Madeira Tourism
p.168 Homem em Pé stones © Madeira Tourism
p.169 Penha de Águia © Matthew Hancock
p.183 Cannon, Pico do Castelo © Matthew Hancock
p.185 Traditional Windmill © Matthew Hancock

Selected images from our guidebooks are available for licensing from:
ROUGHGUIDESPICTURES.COM

Index

Maps are marked in colour